Law Essentials

# MEDICAL LAW

Murray Earle, B.A. (Hons), LL.M., Ph.D.

*Senior Research Specialist,*
*Scottish Parliament Information Centre*

D1354996

DUNDEE UNIVERSITY PRESS
2007

First published in Great Britain in 2007 by
Dundee University Press
University of Dundee
Dundee DD1 4HN

www.dundee.ac.uk/dup

Copyright © Murray Earle

ISBN 978–1–84586–035–6

No natural forests were destroyed to make this product;
only farmed timber was used and replanted.

*British Library Cataloguing-in-Publication Data*
A catalogue record for this book is available on request from the British Library

Typeset by Waverley Typesetters, Fakenham, Norfolk
Printed and bound by Bell & Bain Ltd., Glasgow

Law Essentials

# MEDICAL LAW

# CONTENTS

# TABLE OF CASES

*Page*

# TABLE OF STATUTES

This publication is based on material in M Earle and N R Whitty, "Medical Law" in *The Laws of Scotland: Stair Memorial Encyclopaedia*, Reissue (Butterworths, 2006). As such, the author would like to thank Professor Niall R Whitty (as co-author of the original work) and the Law Society of Scotland (as copyright holder) for their permission to make use of the material.

# 1  INTRODUCTION

## SCOPE

Medical law has been acknowledged as a legal specialism since the 1970s, with the Law Society recognising accredited specialists in the subject. The scope of the specialism is fluid, in so far as several branches of law fall within its remit. In essence, the subject is concerned with the legal interaction between medical practitioner and patient.

## INCLUSIONS

Actions were at one time limited to allegations of medical negligence, which remains the backbone of the discipline. Yet the field encompasses more than actions in negligence, or litigation at all. Where the matter is a legally regulated one involving the human body and medical or biological science, it falls within medical law. If, for example, one considers the beginning of life, subjects within the medical law field will include abortion, sterilisation and control of fertility, wrongful life and wrongful birth. Issues at the end of life may include euthanasia, assisted suicide and ownership of body parts.

## EXCLUSIONS

Having defined the area in this way, it may seem that it is a very large field. But it can be distinguished from other branches of law. It does not usually cover matters relating to medicines, except in so far as the administration of medicines may lead to harm, which may lead to an action in negligence. Even so, products liability will be considered in this book. Neither does it cover health care law or health services law, other than in similar circumstances. The structure of the National Health Service, resource allocation and the delivery of health care are subjects worthy of a separate book.

## MEDICAL LAW IN CONTEXT

The principles on which medical law operates did not, as the discipline did, emerge in the 1970s. For example, medical negligence draws on professional negligence, which itself draws on the law of negligence in general, all of which have a long history. Another example is abortion, which forms part of the criminal law. Existing principles have been gathered together under a single banner.

Arguably, ethics is what links those legal categories involving the disciplines of both law and medicine. Ethical codes may be iterated in the courts, laid down by professional bodies such as the General Medical Council or set out in statute by Parliament. These ethical codes may either drive or be driven by legal developments. Professional ethics and law are not always in accord with one another. The British Medical Association recognises this in *Good Medical Practice*. Professional ethics and law may be in agreement (eg duty of care in negligence) or in conflict (eg therapeutic privilege). Ethics may pre-empt law (eg artificial procreation and transplantation) or vice versa (eg information disclosure requirements).

## PRIVATE LAW

Medical law combines aspects of private law under its banner. It is also inherently comparative. For example, the case law on consent has drawn heavily on the law in the United States of America, Canada and Australia, if only to exclude those regimes. For the most part, Scots medical law draws on or has developed alongside English medical law. While the legal positions north and south of the Border are broadly similar, some differences have emerged over the years, primarily because civil law has been allowed to develop separately under the Act of Union of 1707. It has also been recognised, both implicitly and explicitly, that cross-border differences that may lead to "bio-tourism" should be discouraged. This was one of the principles on which the devolution settlement was built: that it would be inappropriate that people should move from England to Scotland or from Scotland to England in order to take advantage of a different regime. This is particularly true of issues such as abortion, *in vitro* fertilisation and medically assisted suicide.

Possibly the best example of a cross-border exchange is the law of negligence. The law has been similar in the two jurisdictions since the 1950s, when the test of the standard of care was laid down by the Court of Session in *Hunter* v *Hanley* (1955). The test was adopted in a modified form by English courts a few years later, in *Bolam* v *Friern Hospital Management Committee* (1957) and modified again by Scottish courts in *Moyes* v *Lothian Health Board* (1990).

Differences that have emerged are small, yet arguably important. For example, the law on legal capacity and guardianship is different as regards capacity and consent, and breach of confidence is an equitable wrong in

England but a delict in Scotland. In Scots law, an action for wounded feelings may be considered a personality right, while there is no recourse to the *action iniuriarum* in England. Property law is another aspect of private law that falls within medical law. Principles of property law may be brought to bear on cases in which ownership and possession of body parts are concerned.

## HUMAN RIGHTS LAW

Some commentators have considered with approval that medical law is a sub-set of human rights law. This means that the notion of rights is embedded within medical law because of the latter's dependence on ethics for its development. That said, the European Convention on Human Rights and the Human Rights Act 1998 have had a horizontal effect on medical law, not least because it is unlawful for a public authority to act in a way which is incompatible with a Convention right under the Human Rights Act 1998, s 6. Although the whole effect of the 1998 Act has yet to be seen, it is already clear that it has a direct effect on confidentiality and public disclosure of private information.

## MEDICAL LAW: RESERVED OR DEVOLVED?

Section 30 of the Scotland Act 1998 deals with the legislative competence of the Scottish Parliament. It refers to Pt II of Sch 5, which lists "specific reservations", so defining those powers reserved to Westminster. The general rule is that matters are devolved unless they are reserved by the Scotland Act. Under Sch 5, the law on human fertilisation; regulation of the medical professions; xenotransplantation; embryology; surrogacy and genetics; and medicines and poisons is reserved to Westminster and cannot be changed by the Scottish Parliament. Similarly, data protection is reserved. This affects access to medical records. Intellectual property is similarly reserved, affecting cloning and ownership of cell lines. Consumer protection is the branch of law dealing with (medical and other) products liability. This area is also reserved to Westminster. These constitutional differences will be noted in relevant parts of this book.

## THE NATIONAL HEALTH SERVICE IN SCOTLAND

The statutory basis of the National Health Service in Scotland (NHSiS) is set out in the National Health Service (Scotland) Act 1978. It requires the Scottish Ministers to promote a comprehensive integrated health service geared towards the improvement of the physical and mental health of the people of Scotland. Services are to be free except where expressly provided for under the National Health Service (Scotland) Act 1978, s 1(2), as amended.

Under the same Act, Ministers are under a duty to promote good health. This falls outwith the scope of this book except in so far as the professions working within the NHSiS are covered in Chapter 2 and it is the health service that will be vicariously liable for the actions of medical practitioners in its employ (eg negligence), will perform the services allowed under certain enactments (eg *in vitro* fertilisation and surrogacy) and will perform the functions allowed under the common law (eg acting in the best interests of the *incapax*).

# 2 MEDICAL AND ALLIED PROFESSIONS

## STATUTORY CONTROL

Regulation of the health care professions is effected by a large body of statute, which is itself an area reserved to Westminster, with some minor exceptions on suitable experience and vocational training (Scotland Act 1998, s 6(1) and Sch 5, s G2). The broad aim is public protection. The relevant professions which are regulated include doctors, dentists, nurses, pharmaceutical chemists, opticians, dispensers of hearing aids, and certain professions allied to medicine. These are all discussed separately.

While there is no bar on providing healing services, the legislation seeks to ensure that those holding themselves out as having a particular skill should be subject to a system of licensing and testing of their competence. Degrees of professional control differ. At the extreme end, it is an offence to practise as a registered dentist or medical practitioner when one is not. At the other end of the scale, professional censure may be imposed for unethical behaviour.

Under s 60 of the Health Act 1999, as amended, primary legislation is not necessary to bring new professions within the ambit of the Acts governing the health care professions. This may be done by Her Majesty by Order in Council and includes, for example, modifying the regulation of the health care professions, including professions regulated by the Professions Supplementary to Medicine Act 1960 and modifying the functions, powers or duties of the Council for the Regulation of Health Care Professionals, the list of regulatory bodies and the range of functions of those bodies. Such Orders in Council can repeal or revoke any enactment, amend it or replace it. Some matters remain outside the scope of Orders, such as abolition of an existing regulatory body.

## COUNCIL FOR THE REGULATION OF HEALTH CARE PROFESSIONALS

On the recommendation of the Report of the Bristol Royal Infirmary Inquiry (*Learning from Bristol* (Cm 5363, 2002)), the National Health Service Reform and Health Care Professions Act 2002 created a body corporate known as the Council for the Regulation of Health Care Professionals. Its function is to oversee the activities of those bodies charged with regulation of health care professions. Part 1 of the Act extends to England and Wales only but Parts 2 and 3 extend to the whole of the United Kingdom. Structural reforms of the National Health Service in Scotland were made by the National Health Service Reform (Scotland) Act 2004.

The Council has several functions under s 25. It must promote the interests of patients and the public in relation to specified regulatory bodies, promote best practice in the performance of those functions, promote co-operation among regulatory bodies and formulate and encourage adherence to principles relating to good professional self-regulation.

## REGULATORY BODIES

The following regulatory bodies are required, in the exercise of their functions, to co-operate with the Council:

- General Medical Council;
- General Dental Council;
- General Optical Council;
- General Osteopathic Council;
- General Chiropractic Council;
- Royal Pharmaceutical Society of Great Britain;
- Nursing and Midwifery Council;
- Health Professions Council; and
- any other regulatory body established by an Order in Council under s 60 of the Health Act 1999.

## DUTIES AND POWERS OF THE COUNCIL

Under 26 of the National Health Service Reform and Health Care Professions Act 2002, the Council has wide discretion in the performance of its functions. An exception exists in relation to an individual whose case is before a committee of a regulatory body, or where an allegation has been made to that committee, for example the Disciplinary Committee of the General Medical Council. In this circumstance, the Council may not do anything.

Otherwise, the Council may, for example, investigate and report on the performance by each regulatory body and on how the performance of such functions compares. It may also recommend changes to the practices of regulatory bodies.

Scottish Ministers and the Secretary of State may ask the Council for advice, which the Council must provide.

The Council may, on the basis of public protection, give directions requiring a regulatory body to make certain rules. These are sent to the Secretary of State and laid before both Houses of Parliament. Under s 28 of the 2002 Act, the regulatory body must comply with the directions, which may include provision for the investigation by the Council of complaints made to it about how a regulatory body has exercised its functions.

If the Council considers that a decision made by a Disciplinary Committee of one of the regulated bodies has been unduly lenient or should not have been made (in the interests of public protection), the Council may refer the case to the relevant court under s 29 of the 2002 Act. In Scotland that means the Court of Session. Referral must be made within 4 weeks of the last date on which the practitioner had the right to appeal against the decision. The court will treat the case as an appeal by the Council against the decision in question. It may dismiss the appeal; allow it and quash the relevant decision; make a substitute decision; or remit the case to the committee for disposal.

## MEDICAL PRACTITIONERS

The medical profession is self-regulating, under the auspices of the General Medical Council (GMC). However, this is set to change if the recommendations of a Government White Paper are put into effect. Under the proposals, the GMC will continue to set standards and remain responsible for investigating allegations of professional misconduct, but adjudication of such allegations will fall to an independent tribunal.

### Registration and qualification

#### The General Medical Council

The GMC is a body corporate. It was established in 1858 to oversee training in and practice of medicine. It is regulated under the Medical Act 1983. Its constitution is set out in the General Medical Council (Constitution) Order 2002. Nineteen members make up the Council, elected from constituencies in the United Kingdom (such as Scotland). Members must be registered with the Council. Other members are appointed by universities and bodies conferring medical qualifications (five) and nominated lay members (fourteen), at least one of which must represent Scotland. The Council may appoint committees or panels to undertake particular functions, including investigation and disciplinary roles. Those in existence include the Education and Investigation Committees, and the

Interim Orders, Registration Decisions, Registration Appeals and Fitness to Practise Panels.

## Registration and liability of unregistered practitioners

Any person may practise medicine or surgery – but not anatomy (under the Anatomy Act 1984) – regardless of qualification. What is unlawful is wilfully and falsely holding oneself out to be a registered medical practitioner (eg physician, medical doctor, licentiate in medicine and surgery, Bachelor of Medicine, surgeon, general practitioner, etc). Unregistered practitioners may not fall foul of the law, if they do not hold themselves out as registered medical practitioners and do not contravene provisions on medicinal products or controlled drugs. Further, according to the Cancer Act 1939, an unqualified practitioner may not advertise a treatment for cancer.

What amounts to holding oneself out under the Medical Acts has been discussed by the courts. In *Younghusband* v *Luftig* (1949), the court found that the accused had not in fact claimed one of the qualifications mentioned in the legislation, by using the designation "MD Berlin" to denote his degree from that university. In *Wilson* v *Inyang* (1951) the court found that it would be a defence that the accused held a genuine belief of entitlement to hold himself out as a doctor. Although unregistered practitioners may not hold appointments at hospitals, an exception exists for non-Commonwealth citizens who are medically qualified in their home countries.

Different provisions exist for dentists and opticians. The "holding out" provisions in the Dentists Act 1984 and the Opticians Act 1958 do not use the terms "wilfully and falsely" and so do not require *mens rea*.

Where the conduct of an unregistered practitioner leads to the harm of a patient, that practitioner may be liable to criminal or civil redress. Death may amount to murder in cases of wicked recklessness (eg administering a substance of unknown chemical properties); it may also amount to culpable homicide. Negligently causing harm would be judged by the standard of a medical practitioner where the defender held himself out as such. Lack of skill amounts to fault in the law of delict. Much will depend on whether the patient knew of the practitioner's lack of registration. Indeed, in *Dickson* v *Hygienic Institute* (1910), it was said *obiter* that an unregistered practitioner, who the patient did not know was unregistered, must attain that standard expected of a registered practitioner.

The GMC Registrar is to maintain and publish up-to-date registers of all registered medical practitioners. The main register is divided into different lists, such as the principal list, a visiting overseas doctors list and a visiting European Economic Area practitioners list. Overseas practitioners are eligible for limited registration which is tied to their employment in the United Kingdom and may be converted to full registration. Provisional registration is available to those with recognised qualifications pursuing further training. They may work in recognised hospitals as if fully registered, but may not undertake certain work.

Practitioners pay an annual fee for inclusion on the list and are entitled to a certificate of registration. Retired practitioners may remain on the register even after retirement.

Entries in the register which, in the view of the GMC, were fraudulently or incorrectly made may be erased at the direction of the GMC. The person whose name was erased must be notified and has a right of appeal.

### Training, qualifications and experience

The Education Committee of the GMC supervises the granting of medical qualifications. It determines the veracity of qualifying examinations and the appropriate level of proficiency. It also ensures that the required post-graduation training is adequate (pre-registration experience or graduate clinical training). The committee may appoint visitors to the medical schools charged with gathering course, teaching and examination details. Institutions offering pre-registration experience may also be inspected.

Medical practitioners should have both a primary qualification (eg degree of Bachelor of Medicine or of Bachelor of Surgery or membership of the Royal College of Surgeons) and a qualification of experience (clinical experience in an approved hospital or institution).

Primary qualifications are gained by passing the examinations of one of the bodies on the approved list, set out in statute. The Scottish universities included are those of Aberdeen, Dundee, Edinburgh and Glasgow. A primary qualification may be acceptable if obtained from a university in the European Union, provided that the GMC Registrar is satisfied as to equivalence. Alternatively, the Registrar may be satisfied by evidence of the qualification being accompanied by a certificate, of having lawfully engaged in the practice of medicine, from the medical authorities of the Member State. Practitioners disqualified in their home state are not entitled to registration in the United Kingdom. Disqualification will be on the grounds of the commission of a criminal offence or professional misconduct. Appeals against disqualification may be made to the GMC.

Qualifications of experience must be in a "resident medical capacity" or in an approved medical practice. Experience gained in other institutions may be counted following application to the GMC. Qualifications of experience must also be for a prescribed time period in at least two branches of medicine, as set out by the GMC Education Committee. On completion, the body issuing that candidate's primary qualification must issue a certificate of completion. Further provisions apply to provisional and limited registration of candidates from non-UK countries (Medical Act 1983, ss 15A and 22).

The European Specialist Medical Qualifications Order 1995 provides for recognition in the United Kingdom of specialist medical qualifications awarded elsewhere. The GMC and the specialist training authority of the Royal Colleges are designated for the United Kingdom in relation to specialist medical qualifications. These two authorities award certificates to those who have completed approved specialist training. The GMC publishes a register of such specialists. This is required for employment as a consultant in the National Health Service. Appeals may be made to a panel of independent persons, which must give reasons for its decision.

The Postgraduate Medical Education and Training Board comprises two statutory committees: the Training Committee and the Assessment Committee. The Board is responsible for the establishment and maintenance of postgraduate training in the United Kingdom. It sets the standards and requirements for a doctor to be awarded a certificate of completion of training as a general practitioner or as a specialist. This must comply with the minimum set out in the Medical Directive (ie EC Directive 93/16). The Board may also appoint visiting panels to visit persons or institutions involved in postgraduate medical education and training. Appeals against decisions of the Board may be made to an appeal panel; appeals from a decision of the panel can be made to a sheriff.

### The medical registers

The GMC must maintain and publish a general practitioner and a specialist register. Copies and information must be provided to those making enquiries as to whether a person's name is included in the registers. A name may be removed in prescribed circumstances, such as when a person ceases to be a registered medical practitioner. Inclusion in one of these registers is required in order to practise as a general practitioner or consultant in the National Health Service in the United Kingdom. A decision by the Council not to include a person's name is subject to a right of appeal under the Medical Act 1983.

Overseas practitioners, such as those who are European Economic Area (EEA) medical practitioners, are entitled to full registration, subject to certain criteria. The Registrar must be satisfied that they hold equivalent qualifications and are of good character. In the case of qualifications gained outside the EEA, regard must be had to acceptance of their qualification by another EEA state. Registration may be full, or provisional in the case of practitioners undertaking employment intended to qualify for full registration. Demonstrating proficiency in English is no longer required.

Limited registration is available on the basis of demonstration of knowledge, skill and experience, depending on the post for which registration is sought. This may be converted to full registration on demonstration of good character and being deemed to have the necessary knowledge, skill and experience. In determining whether to grant full registration to a doctor with acceptable overseas qualifications, the GMC need not make a comparison with a hypothetical European Union equivalent applicant: *R* v *General Medical Council, ex p Virik* (1996).

Temporary registration is open to visiting EEA practitioners. They may practise without going through the formalities of registering an EEA qualification. They must provide the GMC Registrar with details of the services to be provided, and the period for which those services will be provided. A certificate from the EEA authority, entitling them to practise in that country, must also be provided, as must evidence of the practitioner's primary qualification. These provisions enable any practitioner satisfying the requirements to practise, but are limited to specialists. Temporary full registration may be granted, but for up to 12 months only and on provision of evidence of an acceptable overseas qualification; possession of specialist knowledge and skill in a particular branch of medicine; and good character.

A medical practitioner may apply to have his name removed from the register, but restoration requires the approval of the Council or of one of the statutory committees.

## Licence to practise

A medical practitioner may be granted a licence to practise when first registered. The GMC may make regulations as to granting or refusing such certificates, and for revalidation of certificates. The GMC may also publish guidance on the issue of certificates. Appeals may be made to a Registration Appeals Panel.

## Conduct of practitioners

The committee structure of the GMC is important in the regulation of the medical profession, in particular the existence of the Education Committee, Interim Orders Panels, Registration Decisions Panels,

Registration Appeals Panels, the Investigation Committee and the Fitness to Practise Panels. Appeals against decision of these bodies are to the Court of Session or the sheriff in whose sheriffdom the address in the register is situated.

### Committees and proceedings of the General Medical Council
The GMC makes procedural rules for three committees and panels dealing with the conduct of practitioners, including the administration of oaths. These are the Investigation Committee, Interim Orders Panels and Fitness to Practise Panels. According to Sch 4 to the Medical Act 1983, proceedings are similar to those in the Court of Session in so far as warrants may be granted for the citation of witnesses, procurement and recovery of documents and the taking of evidence. If, during proceedings, a Fitness to Practise Panel finds that a matter should be investigated by the Investigation Committee or another Fitness to Practise Panel, direction must be given to that effect to the Registrar, who will refer it to the appropriate committee or panel.

The Council may make rules as to the assessment, by the Investigation Committee, Interim Orders Panels and Fitness to Practise Panels, of the standard of professional performance. These rules may also specify circumstances in which such assessments may be made. A sheriff may issue a warrant if satisfied that it will be required for carrying out the assessment. The Council may also make rules as to the discharge of its functions in respect of fraud or error in relation to registration. It is possible to appoint an assessor to the committee or panels to advise on matters of law.

### Fitness to practise
Among the powers of the GMC is the provision of advice on standards of professional conduct, performance and ethics of members of the medical profession. If an allegation of impaired performance of a registered medical practitioner is made, this must be investigated by the Investigation Committee. That committee decides whether the case should be referred to a Fitness to Practise Panel. According to s 35C of the Medical Act 1983, grounds of "impairment" include misconduct; deficient professional performance; criminal conviction; and adverse physical or mental health.

If the Panel finds fitness impaired, it may direct that the person's name be erased from the register (except health cases), registration suspended, or registration rendered conditional on compliance with conditions the Panel imposes in the interest of public protection or the practitioner's interests. If the Panel finds that fitness was not impaired, it may still give a warning.

Where a practitioner's name had been erased from the register, the Panel may direct that it be restored.

The decision may be appealed. Appealable decisions under s 40 of the Medical Act 1983 are:

- directions by the Panel for erasure, suspension or conditional registration;
- directions suspending indefinitely the right to make further applications for the restoration of a name to the register;
- a decision of the GMC directing that, where an application for the termination of a prohibition has been refused, the right to make further applications be suspended indefinitely; and
- a decision by the GMC for erasure.

Appeals must be made to the Court of Session within 28 days, or to a sheriff in the case of a decision for erasure made by the GMC. The Council may appear as the respondent. On appeal from a Fitness to Practise Panel, the court may dismiss the appeal; allow the appeal and quash the direction; make a substitute direction or variation; or remit the case to the Registrar, who will refer the case to a Fitness to Practise Panel for disposal according to the court's directions.

Following an appeal from a Council decision, the sheriff may dismiss the appeal; allow it and quash the direction; or remit the case to the Council for disposal.

Both courts may make any costs order they think fit.

The grounds on which fitness to practise may be regarded as impaired are:

## (1) Misconduct

The same principles apply to misconduct and to serious professional misconduct. The definition is fairly open. Any "reprehensible conduct" may be included, which creates problems of definition. It remains important to draw a distinction between the private and the public parts of a practitioner's life and not judge the practitioner by the former. There has been much judicial activity around the public/private dichotomy, in particular whether serious professional misconduct hearings should take place in public or in private (see *R (Howard)* v *Secretary of State for Health*; *R (Wright-Hogeland)* v *Secretary of State for Health* (2003)).

What remains important is that patient care, treatment and safety are paramount. The same principle applies to medical practitioners and to chief executives of NHS Trusts. In *Daly* v *General Medical Council* (1952) the Chief Executive, who was also a practitioner, had a duty in both capacities, and in *Roylance* v *General Medical Council (No 2)* (2000) a Chief Executive was found guilty of serious professional misconduct for failing to act over high infant mortality rates and on those grounds to prevent the surgery of a child who later died. A high standard of proof is required in such cases. According to *Lanford* v *General Medical Council* (1990), both the onus and the standard are those of the criminal law. Evidence of the use of indecent language and behaviour towards one female patient corroborated the same conduct against another female patient. This is an example of the use of the *Moorov* doctrine in the law of criminal evidence (*Moorov* v *HM Advocate* (1930)). Evidence of previous misconduct may also be considered, as set out in *Daly* v *General Medical Council* (1952).

### (2) Unethical behaviour

This is defined by codes of medical ethics, which have no formal legal status. Such behaviour may be on the basis of the Hippocratic Oath, or based on published guidelines of the GMC, for example the importance of patient confidentiality, discussed in Chapter 6, below. Breach of confidence may lead to civil proceedings; it may also lead to an allegation of serious professional misconduct.

### (3) Sexual involvement with a patient

This would amount to serious professional misconduct, as discussed above. In *De Gregory* v *General Medical Council* (1961), Lord Denning held that if a practitioner has used a professional position to gain access to family confidences, the same standard must be maintained if the practitioner befriends the family. In the *De Gregory* case, this applied to a practitioner who had an affair with the wife of a family, even although it took place after she ceased to be his patient. It was still found to be serious professional misconduct. Neither would it make a difference if both parties were unmarried. That said, the opposite conclusion was reached in *Nwabueze* v *General Medical Council* (2000).

In *Bhattacharya* v *General Medical Council* (1967), the court held that whether the conduct brings the profession into disrepute will differ from case to case. In that case the appellant argued that the intimate relationship had taken place before the woman had become his patient. Lord Hodson said that a pre-existing relationship may be considered less serious.

Although the penalty will itself depend on the seriousness of the conduct, erasure from the register will be the most likely outcome.

## (4) Neglect of duty

Negligence will be discussed in Chapter 4. Neglect of duty will usually be actionable in civil law, but behaviour amounting to culpable carelessness or indifference to consequences may be "gross neglect" and may lead to erasure from the register. This will constitute serious professional misconduct and may *also* amount to negligence. One example is failure to visit a patient, although this is difficult for the practitioner as he must distinguish frivolous requests. Another example is the failure to supervise medical students properly (*R* v *Secretary of State for Health, ex p Spencer* (1989)).

## (5) Advertising and dishonesty

Advertising may be penalised with erasure, but only if the intention was to attract patients or gain financial advantage. The definition of advertising is straightforward in cases of blatant marketing, but more problematic in a publication in which there is reference to the practitioner's skills or reputation. This may depend on the medium, such that use of the mainstream press to showcase the practitioner's expertise may be seen as advertising. The GMC publishes guidelines which allow practitioners to publish factual information about their practices at local information centres, although the same information cannot be used in the mainstream press (*R* v *General Medical Council, ex p Colman* (1990)).

Dishonesty may lie in claiming payment to which the practitioner is not entitled. Similarly, improper prescribing of drugs for financial incentive may also amount to serious professional misconduct.

## DENTAL PRACTITIONERS

The dental profession – including dentists and dental care professionals – is principally regulated by the Dentists Act 1984 which consolidated more than a hundred years of legislation. The General Dental Council (GDC) is a United Kingdom body. Regulation of the profession is also national. The GDC is charged with the promotion of high standards of education and professional conduct among dentists. The Council comprises fifteen registered dentists, four dental auxiliaries and ten lay members. Members elect one of their number as President.

This is set to change: the GDC constitution will be provided for by Order of the Privy Council. The same will be true of the constitution of the GDC committees. As of April 2007, the GDC agreed that the Council should comprise 24 members, an equal number of lay and professional members and a chair elected from the membership. All members will be appointed by the Appointments Commission, within parameters set by the GDC.

The GDC comprises six statutory committees:

(1) Professional Conduct Committee;

(2) Health Committee;

(3) Investigating Committee;

(4) Professional Performance Committee;

(5) Interim Orders Committee; and

(6) Registration Appeals Committee.

The Investigating Committee considers allegations made against a registered dental practitioner that his fitness to practise as a dentist is impaired. One of the Practice Committees must investigate allegations of professional misconduct referred to it by the Investigating Committee.

Allegations may also be referred by the Investigating Committee to the Interim Orders Committee. In that instance, or if the Investigating Committee refers a case to the Practice Committee or the Registrar, the Interim Orders Committee may impose an interim order. The Registration Appeals Committee will deal with appeals against decisions affecting that person's registration.

According to s 37 of the Dentists Act 1984 as amended, the "practice of dentistry" includes the performance of any such operation and the giving of any such treatment, advice or attendance as is usually performed or given by dentists. It includes operations, treatment and advice on dentures, artificial teeth and appliances and excludes medical tasks carried out by qualified medical professionals.

Unlike medicine, dentistry may be lawfully practised *only* by a registered dentist or visiting European Economic Area (EEA) practitioner, who may practise if entered on a list of EEA practitioners. An unregistered dentist treating a patient may be negligent, but that will not amount to a criminal assault (see *R v Richardson* (1998)).

Certain exceptions exist, however. Dental care professionals undertaking dental work is permissible in the circumstances discussed below, as is dental work carried out by dental and medical students provided that it is undertaken in the course of studies and under direct supervision. This work is no longer, strictly speaking, treated as the practice of dentistry.

It is an offence to practise dentistry unlawfully or falsely to hold oneself out as a practising dentist or to be listed as such. It is also an offence to use the title "dentist", "dental surgeon" or "dental practitioner", or to describe oneself as such, if unregistered.

Dentistry is run as a business in the United Kingdom, with patients drawn from the private sector and covered by the National Health Service. As a business, it is controlled by the 1984 Act, which sets out those persons considered to be carrying on the business of dentistry – that is, a partnership of which each member receives payment for dental services performed by that member, by a partner or by an employee.

The rules set out in the 1984 Act are aimed at preventing persons from employing dentists as a commercial proposition. Corporate bodies may carry on the business of dentistry only if the majority of directors are registered dental practitioners. The maximum penalty on summary conviction is a fine of up to level 5 on the standard scale, although the Professional Conduct Committee may also impose financial penalties of up to £1,000 in the case of an individual and £5,000 in the case of a body corporate.

## Training and registration

Medical authorities permitted to grant degrees in surgery are also allowed to grant licences in dentistry. The GDC appoints boards of examiners to examine candidates for the degree or licence. These are available to those aged over 21 years. Registration is open to nationals of EEA states who hold appropriate European diplomas. Those with dentistry qualifications obtained outside the EEA are entitled to registration if the qualification is recognised by the GDC as demonstrating possession of the requisite knowledge and skill. The holder must also satisfy the Registrar of their identity, good character, knowledge of English and good physical and mental health. Where the qualification is not a recognised one, the GDC may arrange for examinations to be sat. It may also grant temporary registration or registration permitting practice only in particular posts.

Dental authorities must, on request, submit to the GDC information on course content. Visitors may be appointed to visit dental schools to assess instruction given. The Privy Council may be informed by the GDC of shortcomings in educational standards and may direct that the qualifications will not, after a certain date, entitle the holders to registration. This may be revoked if the dental authority takes remedial action. Neither may a dental authority make the adoption of a particular theory of dentistry a requirement of qualification. In these circumstances the authority runs the risk of being reported to the Privy Council, which may withdraw the power to grant certificates.

Dentists must undertake continuing professional training and development during their careers. The GDC may make rules prescribing the training of registered dentists and of anyone seeking restoration to the register. The Registrar appointed by the GDC keeps the dental register. Registration procedure is set out in the Dentists Act 1984, as are the required qualifications. These may be a degree or licentiate in dentistry of a dental authority, a national of an EEA state holding an appropriate European diploma or the holder of a recognised overseas diploma. Holders of such qualifications must satisfy the GDC of their identity, good character and good physical and mental health.

The Registration Appeals Committee makes provision for decisions not to register a person, as well as decisions to remove a name from the register, failure to restore a name and decisions to erase a name from the register.

Decisions of the Registration Appeals Committee may be appealed to the sheriff court, although such decisions made on the basis of non-payment of the prescribed fee are not appealable (s 37). The Registrar is to notify a person whose registration is appealable that the decision against registration is appealable, and must give reasons for the decision. Provision is made as to procedure and applicable time limits and extensions of time limits (Dentists Act 1984, Sch 2A).

Further matters affect both registration and sanction, such as the requirement to have adequate insurance and proceedings following conviction of a criminal offence.

## Insurance

Registered dentists are required to have "adequate and appropriate" insurance in order for their name to be entered and retained on the register. This means a contract of insurance covering possible liabilities in the work of a dentist. The registrar may require any registered dentist to supply evidence of his insurance.

## Criminal offences

A dentist who commits a criminal offence before or after registration may face disciplinary proceedings before the Professional Conduct Committee. This applies whether or not the offence was committed outwith the United Kingdom. The Investigating Committee may refer further matters to the Professional Conduct Committee (SI 2005/2011, art 18), including that the person has:

(1) accepted a conditional fixed offer under the Criminal Procedure (Scotland) Act 1995; or

(2) agreed to pay a penalty as alternative to prosecution under the Social Security Administration Act 1992; or

(3) received an absolute discharge under the Criminal Procedure (Scotland) Act 1995.

Although petty offences are excluded, they may attract professional penalties if part of a string of similar offences which also speak to professional or ethical practice, or which lead to a concern for patient safety.

In *Dad* v *General Dental Council* (2000) the dentist appealed against his temporary removal from the register on the ground of convictions for road traffic offences. The Privy Council set the suspension aside, finding that it was not a question of the gravity of the offences themselves; it was a question of whether the appellant was fit to practise as a dentist. It is necessary and important to balance the gravity of the offence against fitness to practise. There is also a duty on the committee, where practicable, to suspend its determination where police investigations are ongoing: see *R (on the application of Zietsman)* v *Dental Practice Board* (2002), where police investigations were ongoing into suspected fraud by the appellants.

## Professional conduct and fitness to practise

The GDC is required, after consultation, to issue guidance as to the standards of conduct, performance and practice expected of registered dentists, which it must keep under review.

### The Investigating Committee and the Practice Committees

Allegations made to the GDC that a practitioner's fitness to practise is impaired are referred by the Registrar to the Investigating Committee and if appropriate to the Interim Orders Committee. The grounds on which fitness to practise is considered "impaired" include misconduct; deficient professional performance; adverse physical or mental health; and conviction of a criminal offence (Dentists Act 1984, s 27). Matters may be referred regardless of whether they allegedly took place outwith the United Kingdom or when the person was not a registered dental practitioner.

The Investigating Committee investigates the allegation and determines whether it should be considered by one of the Practice Committees (the Professional Conduct Committee, the Health Committee and the Professional Performance Committee). It is then referred to a Practice Committee or, if deemed appropriate, to the Interim Orders Committee.

If it does not refer the matter, the Investigating Committee may issue a warning or advice to the person who is the subject of the allegation. The Practice Committees are required to investigate allegations referred from the Investigating Committee and to determine whether fitness to practise is impaired, taking account of adherence to any published guidance.

The GDC must appoint legal advisers to give advice on questions of law arising in connection with the functions of the committees and the Registrar and may also appoint medical advisers and professional advisers (dentists). It may require the production of details useful to the investigation. This requirement has its basis in the civil law of disclosure. The GDC may seek a court order if the practitioner fails to disclose the required information.

Once an allegation is referred to the Investigating Committee, the GDC must notify the Scottish Ministers and in some instances the person's employer. It may also inform any person, if that is deemed to be in the public interest.

If it is determined that fitness was *not* impaired, the GDC must, at the request of the practitioner, publish a statement to that effect, and may do so with consent of the practitioner. If fitness to practise is found to have been impaired, the Committee may recommend a change to the register, or impose further sanctions on the practitioner.

### Changes to the register

In certain circumstances a person's name may be erased from the register. These include where the entry was incorrectly made or was fraudulently procured, as determined on reference to the Professional Conduct Committee. The person may apply to the GDC for restoration, which may be done through referral to the Professional Conduct Committee which decides the matter.

A Practice Committee may direct that a person's registration be suspended. For practical purposes, this is treated as not being registered. The committee may also end, extend or attach conditions to that suspension. It may also determine that a person's registration should be conditional or that conditions should cease, continue for a longer period or be supplemented with further conditions. It may also direct that registration be suspended. These provisions apply to resumed hearings. They allow a Practice Committee to vary determinations previously made, although the person concerned must be notified.

A person may apply to the registrar to have their name restored, but only after 5 years of erasure and after 12 months of a previous application for restoration. The Professional Conduct Committee considers the application. It may require evidence as to fitness to practise and must be furnished with evidence that the applicant meets the requirements for fitness to practise as regards education, training, good character, etc.

Restoration may be conditional, for example on the existence of adequate insurance or other conditions the Professional Conduct Committee thinks fit for public protection or in the interests of the applicant. Following two or more refused applications for restoration, the Professional Conduct Committee may order that the right to make further applications be suspended indefinitely.

Certain decisions of the Professional Conduct Committee are appealable, for example directions for erasure from the register. Similarly, decisions of the Practice Committees for erasure, suspension, conditional registration or variance of conditions are also appealable.

Appealable decisions may also be appealed to the Court of Session, which may quash the decision; substitute another decision; or remit the matter back to the relevant committee of the GDC.

### General Dental Council sanctions

Following a criminal conviction or a finding of serious professional misconduct, the Professional Conduct Committee may order erasure from the register or the suspension of the dentist's registration. This amounts to disciplinary proceedings on the ground of serious professional misconduct. The standard is that of the ordinarily competent dental practitioner and not the adoption or failure to adopt a particular theory of dentistry. As this is a new provision, any analysis illustrative of serious professional misconduct must be done on the basis of convictions of the Disciplinary Committee (as it then was).

For example, in *Felix* v *General Dental Council* (1960), the appellant, a registered dentist, had been convicted by the Disciplinary Committee of infamous and disgraceful conduct in a professional respect, for wrongfully claiming fees for fillings he had not made and of doing more fillings than were necessary. His defence was carelessness as regards the fees and honestly held professional opinion as regards the need for fillings. As regards the fees, the Privy Council held that it was necessary to prove moral turpitude, fraud or dishonesty, or persistent recklessness as to amount to dishonesty. As regards the fillings, it was held that it was possible that the Committee might have accepted that there had been an honest belief in the necessity of the treatment.

Conversely, in *Carmichael* v *General Dental Council* (1990), it was held that the administration of general anaesthetic contrary to proper practice amounted to serious professional misconduct. The standard applied to serious professional misconduct was similar to that applied in medical negligence.

If fitness to practise is impaired, the Practice Committee may direct:

1. erasure from the register (but not if the sole ground is impaired physical or mental health);
2. suspension for up to 12 months;
3. conditional registration for up to 3 years; or
4. that a reprimand be issued.

The Practice Committee is to notify the person of its determination and of the right of appeal, while at the same time revoking any interim order made. In the interest of public protection, a Practice Committee may also make an interim order, or orders for immediate suspension or immediate conditional registration.

Such disciplinary orders will have financial and career consequences for the practitioner, which should be weighed against the conduct of the practitioner when the matter is considered (see *Dad* v *General Dental Council* (2000)).

## DENTAL CARE PROFESSIONALS

Dental hygienists and dental therapists are known as "dental care professionals" (formerly known as "dental auxiliaries"), as are dental nurses, dental technicians, clinical dental technicians and orthodontic therapists. They are members of professions complementary to dentistry. In order to fall within the definition, the majority of members of the profession must work in connection with dental care and the profession must also be one regulated by the Council for the Regulation of Healthcare Professionals. For example, dental hygienists may carry out work under the supervision or direction of a registered dentist, such as cleaning, polishing and scaling teeth, and placing temporary dressings in teeth; dental therapists may extract deciduous teeth and undertake simple dental fillings, also under supervision.

### Training and registration

The GDC supervises the training of dental care professionals. It has power to appoint visitors to determine the adequacy of instruction and examination. Those in possession of a recognised qualification may be entered on the register, as long as they are of good character. The use of the title of "dental hygienist" or "dental therapist" by one not enrolled as such is an offence that carries a penalty on summary conviction of a fine of up to level 3 on the standard scale (£1,000). The same penalty follows conviction of the offence of using such a title to suggest qualifications in dentistry.

For each of the following classes, the GDC is to determine the appropriate standard of proficiency required and specify the content and standard of education and training (including practical experience): dental hygienists, dental therapists, dental nurses, dental technicians, clinical dental technicians and orthodontic therapists.

The Council may also approve particular qualifications from particular institutions and may withdraw institutions from the approved list in certain circumstances, which may be based on the sufficiency and adequacy of the courses on offer.

Rules must be made requiring registered dental care professionals to undertake professional training and development. Failure to do so may lead to removal of the person's name from the register. It may be restored on application, as long as adequate insurance is in place and training and development requirements have been fulfilled.

The same provisions that apply to dentists' insurance will apply to dental care professionals (Dentists Act 1984 s 36L, added by the Dentists Act 1984 (Amendment) Order 2005, art 31).

Persons registered on the dental care professionals register may be registered only under the titles set out in these regulations. They must satisfy the Registrar as to their identity, good character and good physical and mental health. In addition, dental hygienists and dental therapists must satisfy the Registrar that:

1. they hold approved qualifications;
2. as a national of an EEA state, they have the right to practise as a dental therapist or hygienist in the United Kingdom; or
3. they hold qualifications from an institution outwith the EEA and have satisfied the GDC that they hold the requisite equivalent knowledge.

The registration procedure is set out in rules drawn up by the Council, specifying the form and manner of registration and what will constitute adequate qualifications. The Council may charge a fee for registration, alteration and restoration of a name to the register. Restoration will be possible only if the applicant satisfies the Registrar that the fee has been paid, insurance is in place, the person is of good character and in good physical and mental health and that they have complied with any requirements as to training and development.

The Registrar has certain duties *vis-à-vis* the register. For example, he must make parts of it publicly available and erase the names of those who are deceased. If the Registrar has referred a person to the Professional Conduct Committee and that committee has recommended erasure, the Registrar is to erase that person's name from the register. This may also occur if the entry in the register was fraudulently procured. Detailed provision is made as to appeals (Dentists Act 1984, s 36J and Sch 4A, prospectively added by SI 2005/2011, art 30(2) and Sch 3).

## Fitness to practise

Following consultation with appropriate bodies and persons, the GDC is required to publish guidance on expected conduct and performance of dental care professionals. This must be kept under review. It may differ for different classes of dental care professional. Allegations of impaired fitness to practise may be made on specified grounds similar to those applicable to dentists, that is misconduct; deficient professional performance; adverse physical or mental health; and conviction of a criminal offence.

As is the case with dentists, the Registrar must refer the matter to the Investigating Committee and may refer it to the Interim Orders Committee. The Investigating Committee must investigate and determine whether the matter should be referred to a Practice Committee for further investigation. The Practice Committee is required to make a separate determination in relation to each title under which the person is registered.

The Practice Committee of the GDC has the same powers in respect of dental care professionals as it has in respect of dentists and the same provision is made for resumed hearings, restoration of names to the register, immediate suspension orders, conditional registration, interim orders, recording, the Council's power to require disclosure of information, and notification and disclosure by the Council. These provisions were discussed above, in respect of dentists.

## NURSES, MIDWIVES AND HEALTH VISITORS

### The Nursing and Midwifery Council

The Nursing and Midwifery Council was established in its current form by the Nursing and Midwifery Order 2001. It sets standards of education, training, conduct and performance. Its members serve for 4 years. Twelve members must be registered on the register of nurses and midwives. Twelve "alternate" members may attend and vote when registrant members are unable to do so. The Privy Council appoints eleven lay members representing each country of the United Kingdom. A president is elected from among the members. The Council's four committees are:

- the Investigating Committee;
- the Conduct and Competence Committee;
- the Health Committee; and
- the Midwifery Committee.

## Education and registration

The Council maintains and makes rules for the register of nurses and midwives and for the collection of prescribed fees. Registration is open to those with adequate qualifications as reflected in different parts of the register. Renewal is open to those who complete required continuous professional development and additional educational training and experience.

Nurses responsible for general care or midwives visiting from EEA states are deemed to be registered. EEA nationals may be registered if they have an approved qualification and meet other conditions of registration. Non-EEA nationals are deemed to hold an approved qualification if their qualification attests to an appropriate level of proficiency *or* they have undergone training outwith the United Kingdom to a satisfactory degree *and* have a proficient command of English.

In order to train as a health visitor, a person must be a registered first-level nurse or hold a midwifery qualification and satisfy other specified educational qualifications. Training takes 51 weeks at a prescribed institution. Eligibility depends on completing a training course and passing an examination.

## Fitness to practise and restrictions on practice

Standards of conduct and ethics are made and reviewed by the Council. It may issue guidance and take action if the fitness to practise of a nurse or midwife is impaired through misconduct, incompetence or ill health. In such cases, it may first be considered by the "screeners" and the Investigating Committee. If there appears to be a case to answer, the matter is considered by the Conduct and Competence Committee or the Health Committee. Those committees may order that the person be struck off the register, suspended for up to a year, or be subjected to a "conditions of practice order" or a "caution order". Any person who has been struck off the register may apply for restoration.

Falsely representing oneself as registered is an offence, as is use of the title "nurse" or "midwife" or claiming to have qualifications for those professions. It is also an offence to permit another person to do so, knowing the representation to be false. Other offences include trying to change the register, failure to comply with requirements imposed by one of the committees and for anyone other than a midwife to attend a woman in childbirth, except in an emergency. The penalty is a fine of up to level 5 on the standard scale (£5,000).

## OTHER HEALTH CARE PROFESSIONALS

### Pharmaceutical chemists

#### Organisation and registration

The profession is regulated by the Royal Pharmaceutical Society of Great Britain, constituted according to the Pharmacy Act 1954. It is a body corporate controlled by the Council of the Pharmaceutical Society. It has twenty-one elected and three appointed members.

Holders of recognised qualifications who pay a fee and are of good character are eligible for registration. Qualifications may be obtained from a university or through the Pharmaceutical Society of Great Britain itself. They should be accompanied by practical experience.

Such people are entitled to a certificate of registration. Displaying a fraudulent certificate is an offence carrying a penalty of a fine of up to level 3 on the standard scale (£1,000). Certificates must be returned to the Society upon ceasing membership.

#### Business and premises

Only registered pharmaceutical chemists (and registered medical practitioners, dentists and veterinary surgeons) may carry on a retail pharmacy business – that is, in the retail sale of medicinal products other than those which are on the general sales list. The business may be carried out by individuals, partnerships or bodies corporate. If conducted by an individual, the business must be under the "personal control" of a registered pharmaceutical chemist (as considered in *Pharmaceutical Society of Great Britain* v *Boots Cash Chemists (Southern) Ltd* (1953)). The name(s) of the chemist(s) must be displayed prominently. Partnerships must be under the personal control of one of the partners. Further conditions apply to bodies corporate, such as the requirement that a registered pharmaceutical chemist must manage the corporation and act in the capacity of "superintendent" in personal control of the retail outlets. Certificates must be displayed prominently there too.

Statutory offences exist in the Medicines Act 1968, as amended, relating to fraudulent use of the titles of "pharmaceutical chemist", "pharmaceutist", "pharmacist", "Member of the Pharmaceutical Society" and "Fellow of the Pharmaceutical Society" and to conducting a pharmacy business unlawfully. These carry penalties of a fine of up to level 3 on the standard scale (£1,000).

Premises are required to be registered with the Society and the Secretary of State must be notified. Annual returns must be submitted to the Registrar and an annual fee paid.

## Professional discipline

Professional discipline is undertaken by the five-member statutory committee of the Royal Pharmaceutical Society of Great Britain, but an NHSiS tribunal may also be used. The committee is appointed by the Privy Council and has a legally experienced chair.

If the chair decides that the matter is not serious enough for an inquiry, a reprimand may be issued. Otherwise, he may direct that an inquiry be instituted. A solicitor will investigate and report on the matter. The subject of the inquiry must be notified, as must complainants. Both parties must have access to documentary evidence. Representation is allowed and the hearing is in public.

At the conclusion of the inquiry, the committee deliberates in private. If the allegation is proven, the subject of the inquiry may be regarded as unfit to practise and their name should then be removed from the register. The decision is made public. There is a right of appeal to the Court of Session. The right exists up to 3 months after the decision.

A person whose name was removed may apply in writing for its restoration, giving grounds for restoration. The application must be accompanied by a statutory declaration and two certificates as to the applicant's identity and good character. Account may be taken of the applicant's conduct since his removal from the register.

Grounds on which disciplinary powers lead to removal from the register relate to misconduct and to conviction of a criminal offence by the pharmacist or his employee, a partnership or body corporate relating to carrying out a pharmaceutical business, or by a pharmacist whose name has been removed from the register. Although conviction of trivial offences will usually be ignored, they may be of interest to the Committee if they demonstrate a pattern of dishonesty.

Under the Pharmacy Act 1954 and the Pharmacists (Fitness to Practise) Act 1997, the Health Committee is to consider allegations against registered pharmaceutical chemists of unfitness to practise because of ill health. It may impose practising conditions on a pharmacist or suspend his registration. An allegation to this effect must be investigated by the Council. If the Council finds a case to answer, it refers the allegation to the Committee, which may impose conditions on the practice of the pharmacist, or make an order directing the Registrar to suspend the pharmaceutical chemist's registration for the period specified in the order. The Committee may also make a *conditions of practice order*, but is under a duty to ensure that the conditions are the minimum required for public protection. Appeals appeal lie to an appeal tribunal established for that purpose by the Privy Council.

## Opticians

The profession is controlled by the General Optical Council, under the Opticians Act 1989. The council comprises 28 members representing different organisations, including the Faculty of Ophthalmologists. The Privy Council nominates nine members, from which the chair is elected; it may direct a special health authority to exercise functions in this regard. The Council may make rules for the conduct of dispensing opticians and optometrists. It may also make rules for the carrying on of an optometry business and its employees. The Council approves training and qualifications required for registration. The Privy Council has the power to monitor the exercise of the Council's functions.

### Registration and discipline

The Council maintains registers of optometrists, dispensing opticians (persons who fit and supply optical appliances) and bodies corporate engaged in either business. It also maintains a register of those training as optometrists or dispensing opticians. Registrants must hold qualifications approved by the Council, based on completing a course from an approved institution. Practical experience is also required. Similar provisions apply to EEA and non-EEA nationals as those applying to nurses, midwives, pharmaceutical chemists, etc. For registration purposes, the Council comprises the Registration Committee (for advice and assistance to the Council) and the Registration Appeals Committee (to determine appeals against a decision of the Registrar refusing registration).

By virtue of the Opticians Act 1989, two committees drawn from the membership of the Council ensure the fitness to practise of the profession. The Investigation Committee investigates allegations of impaired fitness to practise. It refers appropriate matters to the Fitness to Practise Committee. The Council may issue guidance on fitness to practise and on document disclosure for the purpose of investigation. The Fitness to Practise Committee has the power to order the erasure from the register, suspension or conditional registration of a registrant whose fitness to practise is impaired. It may also impose a financial penalty. If it finds fitness is not impaired, it may still issue a warning. A right of appeal lies to the Court of Session or in some circumstances the sheriff court.

## Hearing aid dispensers

The Hearing Aid Council was established by the Hearing Aid Council Act 1968 to regulate the profession. The council comprises thirteen members, including a chair. Groups of four members should be capable of representing the following interests or abilities:

- registered dispensers of hearing aids;
- specialised medical knowledge of deafness or audiological technical knowledge; and
- persons with impaired hearing.

The Council organises training and standards and maintains a register of dispensers of hearing aids and employers of those people. It is an offence to hold oneself out to be a registered dispenser of hearing aids and for an unregistered employer to employ a dispenser of hearing aids. Exceptions apply to trainees under supervision.

The Council is charged with discipline of those registered. This is undertaken by two committees: the three-member Investigating Committee and the nine-member Disciplinary Committee. The Disciplinary Committee is chaired by the Chair of the Council and is legally advised. Legal advice must be made available to all parties. Appeal against a decision lies to the Court of Session.

The Disciplinary Committee may impose one of the following sanctions where a registrant has been convicted of a (non-trivial) criminal offence in the United Kingdom or found guilty of serious professional misconduct:

1. admonition;
2. monetary penalty of up to £5,000;
3. suspension of registration; or
4. erasure from the register.

Erasure provisions apply to partnerships and bodies corporate.

## Osteopaths

The profession is controlled by the General Osteopathic Council under the Osteopaths Act 1993 and its four committees:

1. the Education Committee;
2. the Investigating Committee;
3. the Professional Conduct Committee; and
4. the Health Committee.

### Registration

The Registrar maintains a register of osteopaths. Registration may be full, conditional or provisional, depending on conditions satisfied as set out by the Council. These conditions deal with holding a recognised qualification, good character, good physical and mental health and the payment of a fee.

Conditional registration may be open to those without formal qualifications who meet the other criteria and can demonstrate that, for at least 4 years (continuous or not), they have spent a substantial part of their working time in the lawful, safe and competent practice of osteopathy. In such cases, the person may be required to conform to rules made by the Council, pass a prescribed test of competence and give the required undertaking (eg to undertake further training). It may be possible, on fulfilling certain conditions, to convert provisional to full registration.

The Council may make rules that some or all applicants be registered initially with provisional registration and provide for the conversion to full registration, subject to conditions. A provisionally registered osteopath may practise only under the supervision of a fully registered and approved osteopath.

### Proficiency and discipline

The Council must determine and publish the required standard of proficiency as well as a code of practice. This code should set out standards and offer advice. It must be kept under review and may be varied by the Council. An allegation of a failure to comply with its provisions will not in itself be sufficient to amount to unacceptable professional practice, but will be taken into account in any subsequent proceedings under the 1993 Act.

The Investigating Committee, Professional Conduct Committee and Health Committee undertake disciplinary roles. If there is a case to answer and in the interests of public protection, the Investigating

Committee may order the Registrar to suspend the osteopath's registration. This may happen where preliminary investigations indicate any of the following:

1. conduct falling short of the standard required of a registered osteopath;
2. professional incompetence;
3. conviction (at any time) of a criminal offence; or
4. seriously impaired ability to practise due to physical or mental condition.

An allegation may be referred to the Professional Conduct or Health Committees, which may impose an interim suspension order.

Appeals lie to Her Majesty in Council on a point of law only, but in future will lie to the Court of Session.

It is an offence falsely to hold oneself out as registered as any of the categories of a osteopath. Under certain circumstances, it is an offence to fail to comply with a requirement imposed by the Professional Conduct Committee, the Health Committee, or an appeal tribunal hearing an appeal. On summary conviction this offence carries a penalty of a fine of up to level 5 on the standard scale (£5,000).

## Chiropractors

Regulation of the profession is provided by the Chiropractors Act 1994 which established the General Chiropractic Council and its four statutory committees:

- the Education Committee;
- the Investigating Committee;
- the Professional Conduct Committee (PCC); and
- the Health Committee.

The Council may establish further committees and appoint a Registrar. The Council sets the standards required for full or conditional registration as a chiropractor and makes rules for provisional registration for 1 year. Rules may dictate how conditional registration can be converted to full registration, before which the registrant may practise only under supervision.

The Council determines and publishes required standards of proficiency and approved qualifications, with the approval of the Privy Council, and may require further continuous training of chiropractors.

Following consultation with practitioners' representatives, the Council must prepare a code of practice. This should set out expected standards of conduct and practice and give advice.

Allegations of unacceptable professional conduct or professional incompetence must be referred to the Investigating Committee. If there is a case to answer, it will be referred to the PCC or the Health Committee. On the basis of public protection, any of those three committees may then order interim suspension of registration. Following further consideration, the practitioner may be admonished; have their registration suspended; be removed from the register; or have a *conditions of practice order* made. The decision may be appealed.

The Council may also make rules requiring proper practice insurance.

## Professions supplementary to medicine

The Health Professions Order 2001 brings together and allows regulation by the Health Professions Council of the following professions:

- arts therapists;
- chiropodists;
- clinical scientists;
- dieticians;
- medical laboratory technicians;
- occupational therapists;
- orthoptists;
- paramedics;
- physiotherapists;
- prosthetists and orthotists;
- radiographers; and
- speech and language therapists.

The council comprises the following four committees:

1. the Education and Training Committee;
2. the Investigating Committee;
3. the Conduct and Competence Committee; and
4. the Health Committee.

The Council directs the performance of the committee functions. Further functions may be conferred on the Council by the Privy Council, which must be consulted annually by the Health Professions Council.

The Council must keep registers of the different professions under their various professional titles. It is an offence falsely to hold oneself out as registered under any of the professions supplementary to medicine.

Those seeking registration must satisfy the Council of their education, training and qualification. Similar provisions apply to the qualifications of EEA and non-EEA nationals as apply to other health care professions – that is, the holding of recognised equivalent qualifications and experience attesting to proficiency.

The Council must establish and keep under review required standards of conduct, performance and ethics. These are to be designed around public protection.

Allegations of impaired fitness to practise made against a registrant are first considered by the Investigating Committee or by "screeners" (individuals specially appointed under SI 2002/254, art 23). If it appears that there is a case to answer, the matter is considered by the Conduct and Competence Committee or the Health Committee. They have the power to strike off or suspend the registrant from the register. Appeals are to the Court of Session. A person struck off may apply for reinstatement, but only after 5 years. No more than one such application may be made in any 12-month period.

---

## Essential Facts

*Statutory control*

- The medical profession is regulated by a large body of statute and is an area "reserved" to Westminster under the Scotland Act 1998.
- The Council for the Regulation of Health Care Professionals is a body corporate overseeing the activities of the profession in the public interest.
- The other regulatory bodies are required to co-operate with the Council, which may report on those bodies and may refer to the court disciplinary cases made by those bodies.

*Medical practitioners*

- The General Medical Council regulates the training in and practice of medicine, under the Medical Act 1983.
- Only registered medical practitioners may practise under that title; otherwise an offence is committed.

- The GMC Registrar must maintain and publish registers of general practitioners and specialist practitioners.
- Registration is open to those who have completed particular qualifications, and to EEA and non-EEA practitioners if their qualifications are seen as equivalent.
- Training, qualifications and experience are supervised by the GMC Education Committee. Practitioners must have a primary qualification and a qualification of practical experience in a resident capacity.
- Licence to practise may be obtained once registered and this is regulated by the GMC.
- Misconduct leading to the harm of a patient may leave the practitioner open to civil or criminal liability as well as professional sanction.
- The Investigation Committee, Interim Orders Panels and Fitness to Practise Panels deal with conduct of practitioners.
- Allegations of professional misconduct must be investigated and may be passed on to one of the panels if there is a case to answer. Panels may direct that the person's name be erased from the register. Certain decisions may be appealed to the Court of Session.
- Grounds on which fitness to practise may be impaired are misconduct; unethical behaviour; sexual involvement with a patient; neglect of duty; and advertising and dishonesty.

*Dental practitioners*

- The dental profession is regulated by the Dentists Act 1984 under the General Dental Council.
- The GDC comprises six committees (the Professional Conduct Committee, the Health Committee, the Investigating Committee, the Professional Performance Committee, the Interim Orders Committee and the Registration Appeals Committee).
- The GDC Registrar must keep a register of those whose qualifications entitle them to practise.
- The GDC regulates and supervises admissible qualifications and experience.
- Dentistry is run as a business in the United Kingdom. Separate provisions apply to partnerships and bodies corporate.
- Insurance is required of dentists in practice.

- Allegations that fitness to practise is impaired are investigated by the Investigation Committee and may be referred to the Interim Orders Committee while an investigation is ongoing.

- The Registrar refers allegations of professional misconduct to the Investigation Committee and, if appropriate, the Interim Orders Committee. If there is a case to answer, the matter is referred to one of the Practice Committees.

- The grounds on which fitness to practise is considered "impaired" include misconduct; deficient professional performance; adverse physical or mental health; and conviction of a criminal offence.

- In certain circumstances a person's name may be erased from the register – if it was fraudulently entered or following a finding of serious professional misconduct. Under certain conditions it may be reinstated.

- Dental care professionals (dental hygienists and dental therapists) are also regulated by the GDC. Similar provisions apply to registration, training and insurance as apply to dentists.

*Nurses, midwives and health visitors*

- The Nursing and Midwifery Council was established by the Nursing and Midwifery Order 2001.

- The Council has four committees: the Investigating Committee, the Conduct and Competence Committee, the Health Committee and the Midwifery Committee.

- The Council maintains a register of nurses and midwives and makes rules as regards training sufficient for registration; it also makes and keeps under review standards and codes of conduct.

- The Conduct and Competence Committee or the Health Committee may order that a person be struck off.

*Other health care professionals*

- Other health care professionals are regulated by individual regulatory bodies having similar roles to the General Medical Council and the General Dental Council as regards qualifications, registration, conduct and discipline.

- The Councils regulating the various health care professions also comprise appropriate committees for conduct, registration, discipline and investigation, similar to those regulating medicine and dentistry. They may also impose sanctions on practitioners for misconduct.

- Councils must also determine and publish the required standards of proficiency and codes of practice.

- Pharmacists are regulated by the Pharmaceutical Society of Great Britain under the Pharmacy Act 1954.

- Further provisions apply to pharmacists, pharmaceutical chemists and businesses and bodies corporate relating to the role of superintendents, for example.

- Statutory offences including fraudulent use of various titles apply to pharmacists. Similar offences apply to the other health care professions.

- Opticians are regulated by the General Optical Council under the Opticians Act 1989.

- Hearing aid dispensers are regulated by the Hearing Aid Council established by the Hearing Aid Council Act 1968.

- Osteopaths are regulated by the General Osteopathic Council under the Osteopaths Act 1993.

- Chiropractors are regulated under the Chiropractors 1994 Act by the General Chiropractic Council and its four statutory committees.

- The Health Professions Order 2001 brings together and allows regulation by the Health Professions Council of arts therapists, chiropodists, clinical scientists, dieticians, medical laboratory technicians, occupational therapists, orthoptists, paramedics, physiotherapists, prosthetists and orthotists, radiographers and speech and language therapists.

### Essential Cases

**Younghusband v Luftig (1949)**: the accused had not claimed one of the qualifications mentioned in the legislation, by using the designation "MD Berlin" to denote his degree from that university.

**Wilson v Inyang (1951)**: it will be a defence that the accused held a genuine belief of entitlement to hold himself out as a doctor.

**R v General Medical Council, ex p Virik (1996)**: in determining whether to grant full registration to a doctor with acceptable overseas qualifications, the GMC need not make a comparison with a hypo-thetical EU equivalent applicant.

**Lanford v General Medical Council (1990)**: in allegations of misconduct by a medical practitioner, the onus and standard of proof required are those of the criminal law.

**Daly v General Medical Council (1952)**: the Chief Executive, who was also a practitioner, had a duty in both capacities.

**Roylance v General Medical Council (No 2) (2000)**: a Chief Executive was found guilty of serious professional misconduct for failing to act over high infant mortality rates and on those grounds to prevent the surgery of a child who later died.

**De Gregory v General Medical Council (1961)**: if a practitioner has used a professional position to gain access to family confidences, the same standard must be maintained if or when the practitioner befriends the family.

**Bhattacharya v General Medical Council (1967)**: whether the conduct brings the profession into disrepute will differ from case to case.

**R v Richardson (1998)**: an unregistered dentist treating a patient may be negligent, but that will not amount to a criminal assault.

**Felix v General Dental Council (1960)**: to ensure a finding by the GDC of infamous and disgraceful conduct in a professional respect for wrongfully claiming fees, it is necessary to prove moral turpitude, fraud or dishonesty, or persistent recklessness such as to amount to dishonesty.

# 3 FERTILITY, GENETICS AND REPRODUCTION

## INFERTILITY

### Rights and definitions

Infertility may be defined in several ways, and has been by the World Health Organisation and the Human Fertilisation and Embryology Authority (HFEA). For present purposes it is considered to be the inability to conceive despite unprotected sexual intercourse for a period of time.

The right to found a family is guaranteed under Art 12 of the European Convention on Human Rights (ECHR). This may have implications for the provision of fertility services. Indeed, in *R (on the application of Assisted Reproduction and Gynaecology Centre) v Human Fertilisation and Embryology Authority* [2002] EWCA Civ 20, the court assumed that Art 8 (on respect for private and family life) and 12 (the right to found a family) apply to keeping embryos outside the body.

Treatment for infertility may involve one or more of the following techniques: *in vitro* fertilisation, artificial insemination, donated gametes (sperm and eggs) and surrogacy. Where medical technology is employed, the terms of the Human Fertilisation and Embryology Act 1990 come into play. The Act regulates the storage, use and creation of human embryos and the licensing of clinics engaged in those activities.

### *In vitro* fertilisation

#### Human Fertilisation and Embryology Act 1990

The Warnock Report of 1984 recommended that there should be statutory regulation of this aspect of medical practice. The Report was prompted by concerns that increasingly available reproductive technology might be open to abuse. The statutory regulation came in the form of the Human Fertilisation and Embryology Act 1990 (the "1990 Act"). Its terms are reserved to Westminster under Head J3 of Sch 5 to the Scotland Act 1998. As a result, all subordinate legislation and the subject-matter of the 1990 Act are not within the legislative competence of the Scottish Parliament. For this reason, the case law of England and Wales, as well as that of Scotland, will be referred to.

The areas covered by the 1990 Act are:

- access to treatment;
- licensing of practices offering treatment;

- consent to use of genetic material;
- control of information;
- conscientious objection of medical practitioners; and
- status of children born as a result of infertility treatments.

The 1990 Act regulates infertility treatment, and research on and storage of human embryos. It covers only embryos created and stored outside the body. "Embryo" is defined as a live human embryo that has undergone completed fertilisation – that is, where a two-cell zygote has been brought into existence. "*In vitro* embryo creation" refers to fertilisation outside the body, even if fertilisation was not completed there.

"Treatment services" refers to medical, obstetric or surgical services open to the public, to assist women to carry children. A woman is said to be carrying a child only once the embryo has become implanted in her womb.

### The Human Fertilisation and Embryology Authority

The Human Fertilisation and Embryology Authority (HFEA) was created by the 1990 Act. It is a corporate body with a Chair, deputy and members appointed by the Secretary of State, most of whom must be neither doctors nor scientific researchers. The Chair and deputy must not be scientists either. The HFEA must publish an annual report and maintain a code of practice. It is also required to keep certain matters under review, such as information on the development of human embryos, and to perform those functions set out in regulations. These are found in various statutory instruments subordinate to the 1990 Act, such as the Human Fertilisation and Embryology Act 1990 (Amendment) Regulations 2006.

The activities of the HFEA are required to be publicised and publicity material must offer advice to those seeking the services that fall under the purview of the HFEA.

### Licensing and licences

Crucially, the HFEA grants licences under the terms of the 1990 Act; "licence" means one granted under the 1990 Act. Three general situations are envisaged:

1. The HFEA grants licences for otherwise illegal activities that are capable of licensing under the 1990 Act. This means that licences may not be granted for illegal activities (such as human cloning) which the HFEA does not have authority to license under the 1990

Act. An example of this category is the storage of gametes and the mixing of gametes of any animal, as well as the creation and storage of embryos.

2. The HFEA does not grant licences for legal activities not requiring licences, such as artificial insemination using donor sperm.

3. The HFEA can not grant licences for activities specifically prohibited under the 1990 Act, such as:

- use for reproduction of eggs from a foetus or embryos created using those eggs. Research using foetal gametes is permitted, however;
- keeping an embryo beyond the "primitive streak", that is, up to 14 days from the mixing of gametes, under s 3(4);
- human cloning, defined as replacing a nucleus of a cell of an embryo with a nucleus taken from a cell of any person, embryo or subsequent development of an embryo.

Licences may be issued by the HFEA for gamete storage and embryo research. The procedure for issuing licences is set out in the 1990 Act. It is undertaken by the Licence Committee of the HFEA, which also has the role (under s 9) of variation, suspension and revocation of licences. That committee is constituted under the Human Fertilisation and Embryology (Licence Committee and Appeals) Regulations 1991.

Licences are issued for specific purposes, to the person responsible for those activities. That person will be the clinician, or the nominal licensee in the case of a manager or administrator of a clinic. Further conditions apply to that person, for example the requirement to keep records of the activities undertaken and provisions as to consents to use of embryos and gametes.

A licence may be granted in respect of infertility treatment, storage and research, but only to be carried out on the premises to which the licence applies. The HFEA may enter and inspect the premises. The activity may not be supervised by more than one person or carried out in more than one place. Certain activities may not be undertaken except in pursuance of the terms and conditions of a licence. These categories (under s 3 and Sch 2) are research, treatment and storage.

## Research licences

A licence for research may be granted to a single person, to authorise activities as part of a single research project over up to 3 years. This may include *in vitro* creation and subsequent storage of embryos for research. The HFEA must be satisfied that the activities will:

- promote advances in treatment for infertility;
- increase knowledge of congenital disease or causes of miscarriage; or
- develop more effective methods of contraception or methods for detecting genetic abnormalities.

Regulations such as the Human Fertilisation and Embryology (Research Purposes) Regulations 2001 may set out further specific reasons for which research licences may be granted, rather than the broad purposes for which they may be granted under the 1990 Act.

Research licences may not authorise those activities specifically prohibited as set out above. Section 15 of and Sch 3 to the 1990 Act set out specific conditions that apply to research licences, for example that an embryo set aside for a research project may be used only for that project.

### Infertility treatment licences

Treatment licences may be granted for up to 5 years, to authorise activities in the provision of treatment services such as the creation of embryos *in vitro*, the placing of an embryo in a woman and determining the suitability of so doing. It is permitted to mix sperm with the egg of an animal in order to determine normality or fertility, but the product must then be destroyed. The treatment licence may not authorise altering the genetic structure of a cell that forms part of an embryo.

Aside from the general conditions that apply to licences as set out above, and those that apply to consent, there are conditions specific to treatment licences. These relate to the requirements on the HFEA to record the services provided, the persons treated and the persons whose gametes are retained for the creation of embryos.

Records should retain details of any child who appears to have been born as a result of treatment. The welfare of the child is paramount in the provision of treatment services under the 1990 Act. Treatment may be provided only if this has been taken into account, as has the welfare of any child who may be affected by the birth of a child as a result of infertility treatment. Welfare considerations include the need for a father. Treatment may not proceed unless the woman has been given proper counselling, or the woman and the man where they are being treated together.

### Storage licences

A storage licence may be granted for up to 5 years for embryos and 10 years for gametes, after which they must be allowed to perish. This period for gametes may be increased in some circumstances, for example where the fertility of a person under 45 years of age when they provided the gametes is likely to become significantly impaired and where their provision is not for the treatment of another person. The increased storage period decreases with the age of the person whose fertility will become impaired. The younger they were when providing gametes, the longer the gametes may be stored.

The storage period for embryos may be increased to up to 10 years (depending on patient age) where each person who contributed gametes does not object, where the woman being treated is under 50 years of age and treatment is not for the purposes of surrogacy, and where two medical practitioners give a written opinion that the woman being treated is likely to become infertile.

Embryos created *in vitro* may not be stored without the consent of the persons whose gametes contributed to the embryo. That consent must be in writing and specify the maximum period of storage allowed, up to the statutory maximum. Embryos must be stored according to the terms of that consent and the conditions of the licence. The HFEA Code of Practice makes further provision for storage licences. Although the 7th edition is currently in development, the 6th edition was altered in the course of its own development, to take account of the situation in which a woman's embryos were destroyed without her knowledge or consent after her former husband withdrew his consent to their storage. The amendment specifies that where one person withdraws consent, the HFEA should take steps to inform the other.

Gametes stored may be only those to which a licence applies. An embryo created *in vitro*, not under a licence, may be stored only if it was acquired from a person to whom a licence applies. Where gametes or embryos have been stored, they may not be supplied unless for the provision of treatment services to a person to whom a licence applies.

### Pre-implantation genetic diagnosis licences
The technology behind pre-implantation genetic diagnosis (PGD) allows the screening of embryos for genetic characteristics, including sex selection which is contrary to the HFEA Code of Practice. PGD requires a licence. It involves selecting those embryos that are implanted in the uterus.

While screening out embryos on the basis of sex alone is contrary to the Code, certain so-called X-linked hereditary conditions that are suffered only by members of a particular sex may be screened out. Examples include Duchene muscular dystrophy, which is a debilitating condition suffered by males.

In *R (Quintavalle)* v *Human Fertilisation and Embryology Authority* (2005), sex selection was allowed using PGD, to ensure that the child born would be a suitable bone marrow donor for his brother, who had a genetic form of anaemia. The family also sought a child who would not inherit the condition. The HFEA was prepared to grant a licence only for the diagnosis of the genetic condition, rather than for the tissue typing. Under judicial review of that decision, the House of Lords held that the case hinged on the meaning of "suitability" under s 2(1) of the 1990 Act. Tissue typing through PGD and IVF may allow a woman to be less inhibited about bearing children; the Act therefore allowed the HFEA to grant such a licence. The HFEA subsequently amended its Guidelines.

## Consent

Consent is fundamental to the storage and use of gametes and embryos, particularly with regard to the concept of being "treated together", which is discussed further below. Schedule 3 to the 1990 Act sets out what is required for consent to be valid. These requirements are more stringent than common law provisions as to consent of donors and recipients of genetic material. An example of the greater stringency is in the requirement to provide counselling services. The HFEA Code of Practice gives some guidance but does not carry the force of law. The consents required under s 25 of the 1990 Act for licensing, storage and use ensure that legal control of the genetic material remains with the suppliers of that material.

In general, there must be written consent to the use of the embryo, specifying that its use is for the provision of treatment services to the consenting party. The consent must specify that use is for the person treated as specified in the treatment licence, or that person and another specified person treated together. Alternatively, the consent may specify that the infertility treatment licence is for providing treatment services to persons not including the person giving consent, ie in the case of donated gametes. The records that are required to be kept in providing treatment services must contain details of the consent given.

As is the case with consent to medical treatment generally, consent here should not be given under undue influence. Although there is no Scottish case law in point, this area was considered by the High Court in England in *Centre for Reproductive Medicine* v *U* (2002). That case involved the use of sperm after the donor's death. It had been surgically removed while U was alive, as he had previously had a vasectomy. Proper consent to retrieval and storage of the sperm had been given and counselling provided. Although provision existed for use of the sperm after U's death, the Centre for Reproductive Medicine had indicated on the form that posthumous conception would not be in the interest of the chid born as a result and was unethical. The Centre had agreed to store the sperm only during U's life, yet on a different form U had specified that it should still be stored for use after his death. He subsequently altered the form at a follow-up appointment with a specialist nurse, specifying that the sperm should be allowed to perish. It was common ground that the nurse had asked Mr U to change the form, yet Mrs U argued that Mr U changed it reluctantly and under the authority of the nurse.

Three embryos were created *in vitro*, two of which were implanted in Mrs U. A pregnancy was not successful and the third embryo was stored. Mr U subsequently died. The Centre argued that the third embryo should be allowed to perish, on account of Mr U's withdrawal of consent to the storage of his sperm after his death, which would make its continued storage thereof a criminal offence.

On the one hand, the HFEA is on record as discouraging posthumous conception; the 1990 Act specifies that in those circumstances a person in U's position would not be treated as the father of the chid and that treatment services should not be provided unless the welfare of the child has been taken into account. On the other hand, Mrs U relied on misrepresentation, undue influence and duress. The Centre sought the guidance of the court. The case law on undue influence was not helpful to the court, as the Centre would gain nothing through the alteration made to the form. The court found that Mr U did not make the changes under any compulsion and the question remained whether effective consent had been given by Mr U to the storage and use of the third embryo. The court found no reason to believe that Mr U had not intended to make the alteration he had made, and the cells should be allowed to perish.

### Storage and being "treated together"

*R* v *Human Fertilisation and Embryology Authority, ex parte Blood* (1997) (the "*Blood* case") and *U* v *W* (1998) dealt with storage, licensing, consent and "treatment together" under the 1990 Act.

In the *Blood* case, Mr Blood died following meningitis. Sperm was taken and stored without his express consent before his death, while he was unconscious. His consent therefore did not specify what should be done with the sperm in the event of his death. The HFEA refused a treatment licence, on the ground of lack of consent, although Mrs Blood argued that her husband had given his consent in informal discussion and that an export licence to Belgium should be granted. The court found that this should be granted under the EC Treaty on free movement of goods and services, as, without it, Mrs Blood would be denied treatment in a Member State.

However, this left the matter of storage, which cannot be done without written consent of both parties. Yet, given that the sperm had already been stored, the question of treatment, too, remained. A treatment licence was refused, as the Bloods had not been treated together. Under judicial review of that decision it was held that the clinic had acted unlawfully in storing the sperm without consent (it was not prosecuted as storage had occurred while the case was under way). With the taking and storage being unlawful and treatment therefore refused, conception by artificial insemination depended on the export of the sperm to Belgium, which was permitted.

The court in U v W had the benefit of the decision in the *Blood* case. U had been successfully treated in Rome, using sperm donated by W. The couple had separated after the birth of twins and U sought a declaration of W's paternity. This would be possible only if the couple were deemed to have been "treated together". The court found that they had been so treated and that the terms of the 1990 Act effectively restricted U's access to services under the EC Treaty. Yet U lost her case, on the ground that the clinic in Rome was not a licence holder under the 1990 Act.

It has been held in subsequent cases that the right to family life under Art 8 of the European Convention on Human Rights does not override withdrawal of consent by one of the parties formerly "treated together" with the other. See *Evans v Amicus Healthcare Ltd; Hadley v Midland Fertility Services Ltd* (2003).

### Cloned embryos

Following the decision in *R (Quintavalle) v Secretary of State for Health* (2003), the 1990 Act was deemed to apply to cloned embryos, despite the argument by a pro-life group that it did not. The rationale of the decision was that Parliament would not have intended to differentiate on the basis of the method of the creation of an embryo. In the spirit of the law, cloned embryos fall within the definition of "embryo" under the 1990 Act, despite fertilisation not having taken place as a matter of science.

### Offences

Under s 3 of the 1990 Act, it is an offence to place non-human embryos or gametes inside a woman. The penalty is up to 10 years in prison or a fine, or both (see s 41).

It is not permitted to keep an embryo after the appearance of the "primitive streak" (14 days). This offence carries the same penalty.

Lesser offences are committed by doing those things requiring a licence, but doing so without that licence having been granted. This includes doing so even where a licence would have been permitted but was nonetheless not obtained. These offences attract a penalty of 2 years' imprisonment on indictment and 6 months' imprisonment on summary conviction.

Under s 41 of the 1990 Act, no money or benefit may be received in respect of the supply of gametes or embryos. It is an offence for any person to whom a licence applies to accept such money or benefit. This attracts a penalty of up to 6 months' imprisonment on indictment or a fine of up to level 5 on the standard scale (£5,000), or both.

## Donor anonymity, maternity and paternity

A list of "identifiable individuals" whose gametes have been stored or used and those who have been treated must be maintained by the HFEA. Anonymity of those who made donations before April 2005 must be preserved, although information on their genetic health and ethnic origin may be passed on where a child was born as a result, but only after that child becomes 18. The donor's identity may be divulged where the donation was made after April 2005, under the Human Fertilisation and Embryology (Disclosure of Information) Act 1992. This information may also be available under Art 8 of the ECHR. A court may order this where there is a dispute as regards parentage or in connection with a congenital disability, once the implications of disclosure have been explained to the donor.

The 1990 Act makes provision as to those who will be regarded as the parents of a child born as a result of treatment under that Act. None, one or both of the parties treated together may be the biological parents of the child, depending on the technique used. The rules set out in the 1990 Act can not be rebutted; they do not, however, apply to the transfer of titles or honours.

The woman carrying the child is considered the mother, regardless of the genetic provenance of the child she carries and regardless of where the woman was treated. Her consent to a subsequent adoption order and the granting of that order would change this position. If the woman carrying the child was married at the time of treatment, her husband is treated as the father of that child. Again, this presumption is regardless of whether it was his sperm that contributed to the embryo she carried until birth. The exception to this rule is where the husband did not consent to the sperm of another man being used, although he will bear the onus of establishing lack of consent. If the couple is not married, but were treated together under the

1990 Act, the man treated with the mother of the child is regarded as the child's father. This rule does not apply to same-sex couples and has several additional conditions attached to it, such as that the treatment must have been provided by a clinic licensed by the HFEA.

## Control of information

This area of coverage of the 1990 Act refers to the requirement for the HFEA to maintain a register of storage and treatment services provided. It must also maintain a register of any identifiable individuals born as a result of services offered under the 1990 Act. The information is gathered by clinics as licence holders and passed to the HFEA. These registers become important, given the legal position on paternity. It is also important because once a child conceived by the techniques regulated by the HFEA reaches the age of 18, the identity of their biological father may be made available to them. It may also be possible to get that information on becoming 16, provided that the minor is capable under the Age of Legal Capacity (Scotland) Act 1991. This capacity is discussed further in Chapter 5.

In Chapter 6 we turn to confidentiality and justification for breaches of medical confidentiality. Some parallels can be drawn at this stage. For example, under the 1990 Act, an individual may obtain information on the genetic origins of a prospective spouse where they may fall within one of the prohibited relationships for marriage. Similarly, information may be obtained by a child who sues in negligence, where they were born with a disability following treatment. These are covered by the exception to the duty of confidentiality where information is passed on as a result of legal processes. Other exceptions to the duty of confidentiality, such as consent to disclosure and emergency or necessity, also apply in the 1990 Act, allowing disclosure in those situations.

Information may also be obtained under the Data Protection Act 1998 and the Access to Health Records Act 1990. Similar provisions apply to sharing of health information among HFEA employees as apply to justification for breach of confidence among members of the health care team.

## Access to treatment

The 1990 Act does not place restrictions on access to treatment, although the HFEA is required to take into account the welfare of any child to be born as a result of treatment. HFEA guidance sets out conditions to be taken into account, and has taken the interests of an existing child into account in deciding whether to provide treatment. This followed the case of *R (Quintavalle)* v *Human Fertilisation and Embryology Authority* (2005) in which sex selection was allowed using PGD, to ensure that the child born would be a suitable bone marrow donor for his brother. Decisions to refuse a treatment licence may be judicially reviewed. This has happened, for example, where treatment was refused to a 37-year-old woman where the HFEA cut-off age was set at 35. In *R* v *Sheffield Health Authority, ex parte Seale* (1994), the court found that in making its decision, it was not *Wednesbury* unreasonable for the HFEA to consider the likely effectiveness of treatment.

Under s 38 of the 1990 Act, no person may be compelled to participate in any of the activities regulated under the Act. This allows a medical practitioner conscientiously to object to all or part of the regulated activities.

## SURROGACY

There are two statutes regulating surrogacy. These are the Surrogacy Arrangements Act 1985 (the "1985 Act"), unless the pregnancy was medically assisted, in which case the 1990 Act comes into play (eg donor insemination). Under the 1985 Act the "surrogate mother" arranges to carry a child and give it up after its birth to the person with whom the arrangement was made. She may or may not be the genetic mother, depending on the method of conception used.

### Commerce and regulation

The arrangement made between the surrogate mother and the commissioning couple may be informal or formalised and subject to the controls in the 1985 Act. Financial arrangements or "baby selling" are prohibited under the Adoption (Scotland) Act 1978. The 1985 Act also prohibits financial transactions in respect of surrogacy arrangements made. Nor is any arrangement made enforceable.

Section 2 of the 1985 Act prohibits actions done on a commercial basis, such as acting as an agent in a surrogacy agreement or knowingly causing another person to do so, although surrogate mother and commissioning father will not be subject to criminal liability. It is an offence to advertise surrogacy services, however.

Payment made for the benefit of the surrogate mother is not excluded by the 1985 Act. This begs the question of what amounts to "reasonable expenses". In *Re an Adoption Application (Surrogacy)* (1987), the court found that £5,000 did not amount to profit and the adoption order was granted. It also begs the question of enforceability. In *C and C* v *GS* (1996), the mother decided not to give up the child. The court found that the £8,000 paid to her was paid in expectation that a parental order would follow. On the ground of the security of the child, an adoption order was granted. In the interests of the child, a payment may be authorised after the fact even if it breached the prohibition against commercial transactions. In *Re C, Application by Mr and Mrs X under s 30 of the Human Fertilisation and Embryology Act 1990* (2002), it was held that £12,000 was not unreasonable and could be authorised retrospectively when the parental order is made. Reasonable expenses can include loss of earnings and loss of income support.

## Status of the child

A parental or adoption order is required because the surrogate mother, being the birth mother, is the legal mother of the child and her husband is presumed to be the father. However, if the commissioning father's sperm was used and the birth mother was unmarried, he will be considered the father but will not bear parental responsibilities. Where artificial means of reproduction was used, the 1990 Act comes into play, as will the issue of whether the couple was "treated together", as discussed earlier. Otherwise the matter will be regulated under the Children (Scotland) Act 1995.

If an adoption or parental order is granted, it can specify that parental duties have been surrendered. Applications must be made to the court between 6 weeks and 6 months after the child's birth. The child must, at the time of the application, be living with the commissioning couple.

The 1990 Act provides for parental orders to be made where the surrogacy arrangement was made under that Act. A parental order will give legal effect after the fact to the surrogacy arrangement. Under the HFEA Code of Practice, in order for the order to be granted the child must be genetically related to one of the commissioning parents and the surrogate parents must give their consent. They remain the legal parents until the order is granted, at which point the birth certificate must be changed. A copy of the original may be provided to the child once they reach the age of 17.

In *Re Q (parental order)* (1996), the surrogate was single, the egg came from the commissioning mother and the sperm from a donation. The commissioning father was therefore not the biological father and the couple could not therefore be considered to have been "treated together". It was held that no man could be treated as the father for the purposes of giving consent to the making of a parental order and the commissioning couple would have to apply for an adoption order.

## CONTROL OF FERTILITY

The control of fertility may be concerned with attempts to prevent conception, or methods of ending a pregnancy. Other medico–legal issues associated with the control of fertility apply when something has gone wrong, be it due to imperfect consent or negligence in carrying out a contraceptive procedure. It may, for example, be the case that an action is brought in negligence on the ground that, had a sterilisation been carried out properly, a pregnancy and birth would not have resulted. A claim may be based on "wrongful pregnancy" or "wrongful birth"; these will be discussed below. The issue of the control of fertility also raises questions surrounding the rights of the foetus and foetal research.

### Contraception

The legal controls in place regarding contraception relate to several areas of medical law, including negligence, consent and products liability. Much depends on the method of contraception used, be it through medication, a device or surgery. If the method used is pharmaceutical or a medical device, recourse might be had to the Consumer Protection Act 1987, which will be discussed in Chapter 4 on negligence. It may also, or in the alternative, be a question of negligence in prescribing, or in the provision of warnings of side-effects. This, too, is covered in Chapter 4 and in Chapter 5 on consent. The provision of contraceptive advice and information may raise issues of consent and capacity, including the provision of contraceptive advice to the mature minor (as defined in the Age of Legal Capacity (Scotland) Act 1991) or the adult who lacks legal capacity by virtue of their mental health. This is also discussed in Chapter 5.

Of interest here is the issue of post-coital contraception using, for example, the so-called "morning after pill" or through an intra-uterine device (IUD or "coil"). The English case of R v Dhingra (1991) concerned the insertion of an IUD after intercourse. This led to a pregnancy being aborted and raised questions as to whether there had been a contravention of the Offences Against the Person Act 1861 by procuring a miscarriage. It was held in that case that where the IUD was inserted 11 days after intercourse, the woman could not have been pregnant in the sense of implantation having taken place. Strictly speaking, the 1861 Act does not require an actual pregnancy; the intention is sufficient. By contrast, in Scotland, where the 1861 Act does not apply, the common law crime of abortion requires the presence of a pregnancy.

The court has considered whether the "morning after pill" is an abortifacient and hence that its administration and over-the-counter supply amounts to an offence. Following *R* v *Dhingra*, it was held in *R (on the application of Smeaton) v Secretary of State for Health (morning after pill and abortion)* (2002) that it was not an abortifacient because to be effective, it must be taken before implantation.

## Abortion

The law on abortion in the United Kingdom is set out in the Abortion Act 1967 (the "1967 Act"). Its subject-matter is reserved to Westminster under section J1 of Sch 5 to the Scotland Act 1998. The 1967 Act provides defences to what amounts to the Scots common law crime of procuring an abortion – that is, destroying the life of a foetus. The crime cannot be committed if the woman is not pregnant. Until it was judicially established that impossible attempts could be criminal, attempted abortion was not a crime either.

Under the 1967 Act, procuring an abortion is not a common law offence under certain circumstances. The 1967 Act was amended by the 1990 Act. The effect was that of the four grounds for legal abortion, three can be performed at any stage of the pregnancy. In any event, the termination must be performed by a registered medical practitioner, although the 1967 Act allows for conscientious objection. Two registered medical practitioners are required to certify that the ground relied upon as a defence applies in the circumstances.

Four defences are available up until the end of the 24th week of pregnancy. After that, the first ground ceases to be available. The grounds are:

1. risk to the mental or physical health of the mother or to existing children in the family;
2. a risk of grave permanent injury to the mother's mental or physical health;
3. to prevent a risk to the mother's life; and
4. to avoid the risk that the child will suffer from serious physical or mental abnormality.

## The foetus

The foetus is a human organism after it is considered an embryo – that is, from around 8 weeks after conception until it is born. It is not legally protected unless and until it is born alive. This is important in respect of injuries sustained before birth (discussed later in this chapter) and in respect of research on foetal tissue, which is not regulated under the

Human Tissue (Scotland) Act 2006 (see Chapter 7). Research licences have been discussed earlier in this chapter.

## Wrongful life and wrongful birth

Following a failed sterilisation operation, an action may be raised that argues that, but for that wrong, a child would not have been conceived and born. The case may also involve the allegation that, but for a lack of information on the risk of failure, the pursuer would not have become pregnant and given birth. Such cases may be further complicated depending on whether the child born suffers a disability that sterilisation may have set out to avoid.

Sterilisation itself refers to ending permanently a person's ability or capacity to conceive. This may be accomplished through a hysterectomy or tubal ligation in women or a vasectomy in men. As with other medical procedures, there are risks. One such risk may be that it fails to produce permanent sterility, leading to conception, birth and the costs involved in bringing up a child. That would be the legal harm, although an important factor will be whether the child is born with a congenital disability or not.

The legal actions available are the following:

1. *wrongful conception* or *wrongful pregnancy*. The action is brought by the parents in negligence for failure to prevent the pregnancy.
2. *wrongful birth*: the claim is brought by parents for negligent failure to terminate a pregnancy.
3. *wrongful life*: this involves either of the above two claims, but brought by the child, who is usually congenitally disabled. The claim is for the negligent failure to prevent the pregnancy that led to his birth or the negligent failure to terminate the pregnancy that led to his birth.

### *Wrongful pregnancy*

### The healthy child

*McFarlane* v *Tayside Health Board* (2000) raised questions around whether damages could be claimed where negligence in performing a sterilisation operation led to the birth of a healthy child and, if so, under what heads of damages. The case followed *Allan* v *Greater Glasgow Health Board* (1998), where it was found that there was no reason not to be able to claim for the upkeep of the child, although the decision in *McFarlane* reversed that Outer House ruling.

The McFarlanes had four children. Mr McFarlane subsequently underwent a vasectomy and at a follow-up appointment was told that his sperm
count was negative and alternative means of contraception could be
avoided. Mrs McFarlane subsequently became pregnant and the couple
brought an action in wrongful pregnancy, claiming pain and suffering
and distress at the outcome, as well as the cost of bringing up the child and
moving to a bigger house.

The case for the cost of upbringing turned on the manifestation of
the legal wrong or *damnum* – that is, the invasion of a legally recognised
interest. It also considered whether the couple's failure to undergo an
abortion constituted a *novus actus interveniens* breaking the chain of
causation between the wrong and the harm. The House of Lords upheld
Mrs McFarlane's claim for *solatium* associated with her pregnancy and her
patrimonial claim for the expenses associated with that pregnancy. It was
held that the couple's failure to undergo a termination did not constitute
a *novus actus interveniens*.

However, the House rejected the parents' claim for the cost of bringing
up a healthy child. The decision was based on the societal interest in
balancing the increased cost against the parental benefit of a healthy child
and on distributive justice. It was not considered reasonable for the duty
of care of a health authority to include liability for the cost of bringing up
a child. It was considered morally wrong to regard the birth of a healthy
child as a legal wrong.

### The disabled child

There have been English cases in which defective genetic counselling
led to the birth of a disabled child. The parents have claimed for the
difference in cost between raising a healthy child and bringing up a
disabled child.

In *McLelland* v *Greater Glasgow Health Board* (2001), the expectant
mother had a family history of Down's Syndrome that was known to
the health board, who failed to carry out an amniocentesis to diagnose the
condition in her unborn child. The pursuer underwent a non-diagnostic
screening test which proved negative and so did not have an abortion.
Upon the birth of their son with Down's Syndrome, the couple successfully
claimed damages for the increased costs of bringing up a child with a
disability. The court found that the duty of care in this instance included
averting the consequences of the increased costs of bringing up a child
with Down's Syndrome – a case of pure economic loss. It was also pointed
out in the judgment that while *McFarlane* was a wrongful pregnancy case,
*McLelland* was a claim for wrongful birth.

In the English wrongful pregnancy case of *Parkinson* v *St James and Seacroft University Hospital NHS Trust* (2001), a negligently performed sterilisation operation led to the birth of an autistic child. It was held that the Trust was liable in damages for the additional cost of upkeep of the child until its majority.

The effect of these decisions, and of that in *McFarlane*, is that there is no claim for the cost of bringing up a healthy child, but *additional* costs associated with bringing up a disabled child can be claimed under the heads of wrongful pregnancy or wrongful birth.

### The disabled parent and the healthy child

In *Rees* v *Darlington Memorial Hospital NHS Trust* (2003), a healthy child was born to a visually impaired woman after a failed sterilisation. She sued for the cost of upkeep of the child. The House of Lords followed *McFarlane* and held that the costs of bringing up a healthy child could not be claimed, as the health board had not caused the disability which led to the increased costs. To allow such a claim would lead to a slippery slope in admitting a plethora of similar claims. In any event, there is public provision for meeting the consequences of disability. The claimant was, however, awarded a "conventional sum" of £15,000 in recognition of the legal wrong suffered, which was in effect an award for *solatium*. In Scotland this would, in principle, be covered under the *actio iniuriarum* where the *iniuria* is the invasion of a legal right. This *actio* is discussed elsewhere, in particular in Chapter 6 on confidentiality and invasion of privacy and in Chapter 7 on the ownership and control of human tissue and the "organ retention" cases.

### *Wrongful life*

The wrongful life action is brought by the child born following a legal wrong such as a failed sterilisation or the failure to perform an abortion. The philosophical conundrum is that the child is in effect claiming a preference for non-existence over the disabled existence into which they have been born. The argument would be that had their parents known of an inherent risk or had the treatment not been negligently performed, the child would not have been brought into existence. A further problem is that of proof of causation: it is difficult to see how defective counselling would have caused the defect itself, that is the child's disability.

In the English case of *McKay* v *Essex Area Health Authority* (1982), the child was born suffering from Congenital Rubella Syndrome. His mother alleged that a blood test had been performed negligently. The court, however, found that there was no cause of action, as the child was alleging not that they had been born, but that they had been born with a disability. An obligation to abort would amount to placing a lower value on a child with a disability and a higher value on non-existence. Yet, because the court found there was no duty of care, it did not need to compare existence with non-existence. According to *P's Curator Bonis* v *Criminal Injuries Compensation Board* (1997), this decision would be followed in Scotland.

### Ante-natal injury

Under Scots common law, legal personality is attained at birth. There is in general no delictual claim for injuries sustained before birth unless and until the child is born alive. This is the *nasciturus* principle which states that a child is deemed to have been born when it would be to that child's advantage in private law. While the foetus has rights upon birth, this does not mean that it has rights in the womb, so long as the terms of the Abortion Act 1967 have been complied with.

In *Kelly* v *Kelly* (1997) the father of a foetus sought to prevent his estranged wife from undergoing an abortion. The interdict was refused on the ground that rights accrue only upon birth and a father may bring an action only where the abortion would itself be a legal wrong. It was recognised, however, that there had been a trend towards judicial recognition of foetal rights in *McCluskey* v *HM Advocate* (1989). In that case the foetus was recognised as a person when criminally injured in a road traffic accident. Any action still depends on the foetus being born alive.

### Non-consensual sterilisation

Sterilisation without consent amounts to an assault. This possibility will be elided by consent in broad terms, causing the action to be in negligence, as discussed in Chapter 4. The situation is more complicated where the adult lacks capacity to consent by virtue of their mental incapacity. In this instance, the "best interests" test should be applied.

However, the "best interests" test was excluded from Part 5 of the Adults with Incapacity (Scotland) Act 2000. Under s 47, the medical practitioner primarily responsible for the care of the adult with incapacity has the power to decide what is reasonable for the promotion of the physical and mental wellbeing of the patient. This can be done only after the person's guardian or proxy has been consulted. The adult must not oppose the proposed treatment.

This position should be seen in light of the case law prior to passing the 2000 Act. In *L, Petr* (1996), the power was granted to the curator *ad litem* to consent to the surgical sterilisation of the *incapax*. The *incapax* suffered from autism and opposed the petition. The "best interests" test was applied and the risk of the *incapax* engaging in sexual intercourse was weighed against the risks involved in the operation. On this basis, the petition was granted.

## GENETICS

One of the effects of study into human genetics is increased knowledge of characteristics that can be passed on through reproduction. It raises questions surrounding information provision and consent, as well as questions surrounding the standard of care, privacy, confidentiality and, of course, human cloning. Questions are also raised regarding the operation of the European Convention on Human Rights, as the right to one's genetic identity is asserted there.

### Therapy

Two types of therapy are possible. Somatic gene therapy aims to correct a condition in the person treated. This is done by adding genetic material to the pre-embryo. Germ line therapy, on the other hand, corrects a condition in a person's genetic make-up, with the aim of preventing that person's children inheriting a gene, but will not affect the person treated. This type of therapy is regulated by protocol rather than law, because of fears that the technique amounts to a form of eugenics.

### Genetic information

The discussions in Chapter 5 on information disclosure and consent and in Chapter 6 on confidentiality and privacy are relevant here. In so far as genetic information is a factor in confidentiality, privacy and consent, the same general principles apply as apply in those areas of medical law. Indeed, the Human Genetics Commission has recommended against legislation in this area.

### Civil law and human rights

Cases may be brought in the civil law of negligence, based on an alleged failure to provide a piece of genetic information. For example, *Anderson v Forth Valley Health Board* (1998) dealt with a failure to provide such information, leading to the birth of a child with muscular dystrophy. This fell within the law of negligence.

Genetics and human rights will also play a part in the civil law, in particular Art 8 ECHR on the right to family life. In *Re J (adoption: contacting father)* (2003), the mother did not want to tell the father of a child with cystic fibrosis of that child's existence. The court held that it was not in the child's best interests for the father to be informed, hence there was no right to family life in that situation and the child could be placed for adoption.

Further case law concerns paternity more directly, as establishment of genetic paternity will have a bearing on legal paternity. In *R (on the application of Rose) v Secretary of State for Health* (2002), the issue was the point at which Art 8 was engaged where a child was conceived using artificial insemination by donor. The claimants sought information about the donor. The court found that everyone has the right to information as to their genetic identity; thus, Art 8 was engaged.

Other areas of the civil law affected by genetic information are insurance, employment and discrimination law. These fall outwith the scope of this book.

### Criminal law

Genetics in the criminal law is important in expert evidence. For example, *R v Cannings* (2004) concerned Sudden Infant Death Syndrome. Three of the Cannings' children had died without explanation. Expert evidence was led on the probability of three such deaths occurring in a single family. Mrs Cannings was convicted of murder. Her conviction was quashed on appeal once the expert evidence given at trial was undermined. Further evidence suggested a real possibility of a family disposition to the syndrome. Other similar convictions that had been based on the same evidence were also subsequently quashed.

A further use the criminal law has for genetics is in DNA evidence. This has led to cases being re-opened after many years because of scientific advances. This evidence was found admissible in *R v Hanratty* (2002) in the (albeit unsuccessful) attempt to reverse a capital murder conviction from 1961.

## Essential Facts

*Infertility*

- Infertility is the inability to conceive despite unprotected sexual intercourse for a period of time.
- The right to found a family is guaranteed under Art 12 of the European Convention on Human Rights.

In vitro *fertilisation*

- *In vitro* procreation is regulated by the Human Fertilisation and Embryology Act 1990, which established the Human Fertilisation and Embryology Authority (HFEA)
- The HFEA issues licences for certain activities regulated under the 1990 Act, including licences for research, treatment, storage and pre-implantation genetic diagnosis.
- Research licences must be in order to promote advances in treatment for infertility, increase knowledge of congenital disease or causes of miscarriage, or to develop more effective methods of contraception or methods for detecting genetic abnormalities.
- Treatment licences require the consent of the parties treated. Records must be maintained by the HFEA of any child born as a result of treatment. The future child's interests must be taken into account in deciding whether to grant a treatment licence.
- The HFEA may not grant licences for illegal activities such as human cloning, unless this is done for research purposes and the product is destroyed within 14 days.
- Storage licences may be granted for a limited period, which may be increased in certain circumstances such as the health of the donor of the gametes.
- Consent is a fundamental requirement for the storage of gametes and embryos.
- If a couple has been "treated together" under the 1990 Act, the consent of both parties to storage and subsequent use of gametes is required.
- Offences are set out in the 1990 Act. These include keeping an embryo beyond the "primitive streak" of 14 days and engaging in an activity requiring a licence, but doing so without a licence.

- Donor anonymity is maintained in respect of donations made before April 2005. After that the identity of the donor may be divulged to a child born as a result of that donation.
- The legal mother is the birth mother; the father is her husband or the man with whom she was "treated together".

*Surrogacy*

- Surrogacy is regulated under the 1990 Act and the Surrogacy Arrangements Act 1985.
- Arrangements between the surrogate mother and the commissioning couple may be informal or formalised; they may not be commercial, although payment is allowed for reasonable expenses. Surrogacy arrangements will be sanctioned after the fact by virtue of an adoption order.
- The birth mother is the mother of the child, until that child is adopted by the commissioning couple. The same is true of the husband of the surrogate mother.

*Control of fertility*

- Contraception raises issues in negligence, information disclosure and consent, as well as products liability, depending on the contraceptive method used.
- Procuring an abortion is a common law crime. Defences are: (1) risk to the mental or physical health of the mother or to existing children in the family; (2) risk of grave permanent injury to the mother's mental or physical health; (3) to prevent a risk to the mother's life; and (4) to avoid the risk that the child will suffer from serious physical or mental abnormality.
- Wrongful conception or wrongful pregnancy is a claim brought by the parents in negligence for failure to prevent a pregnancy.
- Wrongful birth claims are brought by parents for negligent failure to terminate a pregnancy.
- Wrongful life actions involve either of the above two claims, but brought by the child, who is usually congenitally disabled.
- Courts will allow claims in respect of disabled children to the extent of *solatium* for pain and distress as a result of pregnancy and birth.
- Courts will allow claims for the increased cost of bringing up a disabled child, but not for the costs of bringing up a healthy child.

- Legal personality is attained at birth. There is no claim for injury before birth unless and until the child is born alive.
- Non-consensual sterilisation of an incompetent adult is an assault but this is elided by certification by the person primarily responsible for the care of the adult that their wellbeing will be preserved by the procedure.

*Genetics*

- Genetic information raises civil law questions of information disclosure and consent, as well as confidentiality, privacy and human rights.
- In the criminal law, genetic information is useful in expert evidence.

## Essential Cases

**R (on the application of Assisted Reproduction and Gynaecology Centre) v Human Fertilisation and Embryology Authority (2002)**: Arts 8 and 12 of the ECHR apply to keeping embryos outside the body.

**Centre for Reproductive Medicine v U (2002)**: the case law on undue influence was not helpful to the court, as the Centre would gain nothing through an alteration made to a consent form. That alteration withdrew consent to posthumous use of gametes, which is in any event discouraged by the HFEA and may be contrary to the best interests of a resultant child, which, under the 1990 Act, must be taken into account.

**R (Quintavalle) v Human Fertilisation and Embryology Authority (2005)**: sex selection and tissue typing were allowed, using pre-implantation genetic diagnosis, to ensure that the child born would be a suitable bone marrow donor for his brother, who had a genetic form of anaemia. Because the techniques may allow a woman to be less inhibited about bearing children, the Act allowed the HFEA to grant such a licence.

**R v Human Fertilisation and Embryology Authority, ex parte Blood (1997)**: express written consent of both parties is required under the 1990 Act for storage and use of gametes where the couple is "treated together". Export of gametes was permitted under the EC Treaty articles on free movement of goods and services.

**U v W (1998)**: the couple was deemed to have been "treated together" under the 1990 Act, yet the clinic they used in Rome was not a licence holder under the 1990 Act and hence the claim failed.

**Evans v Amicus Healthcare Ltd; Hadley v Midland Fertility Services Ltd (2003)**: the right to family life under Art 8 of the ECHR does not override withdrawal of consent by one of the parties.

**R (Quintavalle) v Secretary of State for Health (2003)**: the 1990 Act applies to cloned embryos despite fertilisation not having taken place.

**R v Sheffield Health Authority, ex parte Seale (1994)**: it was not *Wednesbury* unreasonable for the HFEA to consider the likely effectiveness of treatment when considering an application for a treatment licence.

**Re an Adoption Application (Surrogacy) (1987)**: £5,000 paid to a surrogate mother did not amount to profit under the 1985 Act and the adoption order was granted.

**C and C v GS (1996)**: in the interests of the child, a payment may be authorised after the fact, even if it breached the prohibition against commercial transactions.

**Re C, Application by Mr and Mrs X under s 30 of the Human Fertilisation and Embryology Act 1990 (2002)**: £12,000 was not an unreasonable payment for a surrogacy arrangement and could be authorised retrospectively when the parental order was made. Reasonable expenses can include loss of earnings and loss of income support.

**R v Dhingra (1991)**: where an IUD was inserted 11 days after intercourse, the woman could not have been pregnant in the sense of implantation having taken place and hence the Offences Against the Person Act 1861 had not been breached.

**R (on the application of Smeaton) v Secretary of State for Health (morning after pill and abortion) (2002)**: the "morning after pill" is not an abortifacient because, to be effective, it must be taken before implantation.

**McFarlane v Tayside Health Board (2000)**: following a failed vasectomy, damages were allowed for *solatium* associated with pregnancy and for the patrimonial claim for the expenses associated with that pregnancy, but the House of Lords rejected the parents' claim for the cost of bringing up a healthy child.

**McLelland v Greater Glasgow Health Board (2001)**: the couple successfully claimed damages for the increased costs of bringing up a child with a disability, following a failure to diagnose Down's Syndrome when it was known the pursuer had a family history of the condition. The case was one of pure economic loss.

**Rees v Darlington Memorial Hospital NHS Trust (2003)**: *McFarlane* was followed in awarding no damages in respect of the cost of bringing up a healthy child born to a disabled woman after a failed sterilisation.

**McKay v Essex Area Health Authority (1982)**: there was no cause of action for wrongful life where a child was born suffering from Congenital Rubella Syndrome following an allegedly negligently performed blood test.

**P's Curator Bonis v Criminal Injuries Compensation Board (1997)**: the decision in *McKay* v *Essex Area Health Authority* (1982) would be followed in Scotland.

**Anderson v Forth Valley Health Board (1998)**: failure to provide genetic information, leading to the birth of a child with muscular dystrophy, falls within the law of negligence.

**Re J (adoption: contacting father) (2003)**: it was not in the best interests of a child with cystic fibrosis that the father be informed of her existence, hence there was no right to family life in that situation.

**R (on the application of Rose) v Secretary of State for Health (2002)**: Art 8 of the ECHR was engaged where the parents of a child conceived using artificial insemination by donor sought information about the donor, as there is a right to information as to one's genetic identity under Art 8.

**R v Cannings (2004)**: a conviction was quashed on appeal once the expert evidence given at trial was undermined. Further evidence suggested a real possibility of a family disposition to Sudden Infant Death Syndrome.

**R v Hanratty (2002)**: DNA evidence was found to be admissible in an attempt to reverse a capital murder conviction from 1961.

# 4 NEGLIGENCE AND CIVIL LIABILITY

The law on medical negligence arguably forms a core element of medical law because, as we will see, the judicial tests for medical negligence are applied to all facets of medical practice. Liability in negligence *per se* falls within the civil law. It is therefore significant that, because civil law was allowed to develop separately following the Union of the Parliaments of Scotland and England in 1707, medical negligence is in some way devolved to Scotland in so far as it has been allowed to develop separately for 300 years. Even so, it is also the case that there are arguably no significant differences between the law in England and Wales and that in Scotland. The reason for this may well lie in the policy considerations that fall in favour of substantially similar regimes north and south of the border.

The law on medical negligence draws on principles of the law of negligence generally and professional negligence in particular. This lies within the law of delict where, in the medical professional context, there may be liability for an act or omission of a medical professional, to the injury of a patient. The burden of proof is on the pursuer to establish that a duty of care was owed, that it was breached by the medical professional's failure to achieve the requisite standard of care and that the breach caused the patient a legally recognised injury.

## THE BASIS OF LIABILITY – CONTRACT OR DELICT?

The conduct of the medical practitioner has long been subject of the law of obligations. There is some debate as to the various roles of the law of contract and the law of delict. Although some institutional writers considered the importance of the principle of lack of skill amounting to *culpa,* Bell's *Principles* considered liability to lie in the implied terms of a contract (eg for the hire of a surgeon). Even some early 20th-century claims lay in contract.

The law in England began to move away from this position in the 19th century, arguably influenced by the fact that a wife had no capacity to contract on her own behalf. This movement towards founding a claim in negligence was followed by the Scottish courts in *Edgar* v *Lamont* (1914). In that case the pursuer injured her finger while gardening. A medical practitioner was called out. The pursuer later sued for negligent treatment and amputation. The defender argued that the action lay in contract and the contract was with the pursuer's husband and hence that, in sending for the doctor, the pursuer had acted as his agent. The court found that liability lay in negligence, regardless of who called the doctor or who the parties to any contract were. As such, liability lies in the breach of a duty of care.

Where there is a contract between the doctor and the patient, a contractual remedy may be sought, although in the context of the National Health Service (NHS), such a contract can be said to amount to no more than a social contract. The terms of the relationship between doctor and patient in the context of the NHS are covered by a plethora of statutory provisions. Claims based on the law of contract will generally be available only to private patients but, for the most part, claims will lie in contract with an additional or alternative claim lying in delict, based on the same set of facts. According to *Roe* v *Minister of Health* (1954), the standard of care in both branches of the civil law is that of reasonableness. According to s 13 of the Supply of Goods and Services Act 1982, contracts for the supply of services contain an implied term to the effect that the supplier will carry out the service with reasonable care and skill. Even so, a doctor may – possibly unwisely – make promises as to the results of, for example, cosmetic surgery. This happened in *Hsuing* v *Webster* (1992). In such a case, a higher standard may apply.

Where there is an available contractual claim, the same levels of damages can be expected and the same rules of prescription and limitation will apply. In both cases the pursuer will need to prove causation.

## LIABILITY AND INDEMNITY

That there has in recent years been an increase in medical negligence claims is not disputed. Neither is the fact that the growth in claims is progressing at a marginally slower rate in Scotland than that in England. Although a claim in medical negligence – whether successful of not – can harm the career of a medical practitioner, it is not the practitioner as an individual who will defend the action or pay the damages. This is because of vicarious liability and NHS indemnity respectively. Liability may also be joint and several and must be covered by an insurance scheme.

### Joint and vicarious liability

*Joint* liability may arise where the acts of different parties contribute to the actionable wrong, provided that they are connected. In successful claims the court may apportion damages *pro rata*, although in practice this does not happen.

Although direct liability is possible, in an NHS context liability tends to be *vicarious*, that is, a third party will be held liable for the wrongs of the medical practitioner. As long as the employee is acting within the scope of his employment, it is the contract of employment between the health service and the medical practitioner that gives rise to the possibility of vicarious liability (*respondeat superior*). The patient may sue the employer or the employee or both, jointly or severally. The NHS will not, however, be held vicariously liable where a doctor carries out private work within the NHS hospital. In such circumstances, liability would be direct.

General practices and dental practices are independent contractors rather than employees. As such, claims are brought against individuals.

In *Bonthrone v Secretary of State for Scotland* (1987), a brain-damaged boy had received the whooping cough vaccine. His parents argued that the vaccine had caused his brain damage. Damages were claimed from the Secretary of State for Scotland (now Scottish Ministers) as vicariously liable for the acts of the general practitioner under the National Health Service (Scotland) Act 1972. The pursuer argued that general practitioners provided services under the Act, which services it was the duty of the Secretary of State to provide. The court rejected this argument and found that the Secretary of State was vicariously responsible for the treatment of NHS hospital patients in hospital, but not for their treatment by general practitioners who should be regarded as independent contractors. However, the pursuer's alternative claim was that the health board (second defenders) were both directly liable and vicariously liable for the conduct of general medical practitioners. The court found that vicarious liability applies only in the context of a contract of employment and hence that vicarious liability did not apply in the case at hand. Neither was the health board directly liable, as it was the general medical practitioner who had administered the vaccine. The meaning and implication of these principles is that employees of a general practice may be vicariously liable.

General practices may be partnerships. As such, the partnership may be vicariously liable for the acts and omissions of its partners. Liability is joint and several for actions within the normal course of the business of the partnership.

## Indemnity

In 1990, doctors working in the National Health Service were given Crown immunity. This means that they no longer need to rely on the services of one of the medical defence societies. It also means that the actions of employees are the responsibility of the NHS.

Since 2002, regulations have established the Clinical Negligence and Other Risks Indemnity Scheme for health boards administered by Scottish Ministers. The scheme provides for the pooling of risks to meet liabilities and does so through members' contributions. It applies to liability for clinical risks in respect of personal injury resulting from diagnosis, care or treatment by act or omission of an employee of a scheme member. Members are not medical practitioners, but the health boards, the State Hospitals, the Scottish Ambulance Service Board, the NHS Education Board for Scotland, the Common Services Agency and the Scottish National Blood Transfusion Service.

The immunity provision that applies to NHS employees does not apply to general medical practitioners, as they are independent contractors. As discussed in Chapter 2, they are still required to take out appropriate indemnity in order to be represented legally at fatal accident inquiries, disciplinary hearings or, indeed, allegations of medical negligence.

## DUTY OF CARE

Even before the House of Lords in _Donoghue_ v _Stevenson_ (1932) cogently set out the standard of care in negligence, Scots law had a mechanism for considering such matters. This was grounded on the neo-Aquilian action based on _culpa_ or fault.

The fact that the doctor owes the patient a duty of care is not a matter of dispute, provided that there is a doctor–patient relationship in existence. Once that level of proximity is established, the enquiry moves on to the standard of care: that is, what duties of care are owed within the doctor–patient relationship.

Although rare, it has been held that a duty of care has been found not to exist, on the ground of legal policy. Examples include "wrongful birth" and "wrongful life" claims discussed in Chapter 3. Where there is no legal interest to be protected, no duty of care will arise.

Neither will a duty of care arise for "pure" omissions, such as in the so-called "good Samaritan" or "duty to rescue" cases. As indicated in _Morrison_ v _Forsyth_ (1995), there is no duty on a doctor to rescue or attempt to rescue a person where the doctor–patient relationship has not already been established and where contact occurs in that context. This is different from the doctor's relationship with his or her patients, where the relationship sets up a duty of care between doctor and patient. Where that duty of care exists, there may be a duty of rescue, for example where a patient suffers from a psychiatric illness manifesting itself in the tendency towards self-harm. This may give rise to a duty of affirmative action.

The notional duty of care concerns the question whether the patient's or pursuer's interest that has been invaded is a legally recognised and protected right, as opposed to a social or moral interest. The duty operates on a threshold basis: the duty not to infringe the patient's recognised interests. An actual duty arises where the doctor-defender owed the patient-pursuer a duty to not infringe those interests in the actual circumstances. For a duty of care to exist, the prerequisite of "foreseeability" must be satisfied: that is, the proximity between the doctor and patient gives rise to foreseeability of harm occurring.

In the unreported case of *Rolland* v *Lothian Health Board* (1981), unforeseeability determined whether a duty of care existed. In that case, the patient became mentally confused and jumped out of a hospital window, to his injury. He was suffering from a psychiatric condition. The health board escaped liability because it was held that the irrational act was not reasonably foreseeable. This indicates that the enquiry into the duty of care is linked with the enquiry into the standard of care.

According to the judgment in *Fairlie* v *Perth and Kinross Healthcare NHS Trust* (2004), in general, the duty of care is owed only to a doctor's patients. This includes circumstances in which a patient's psychiatric injuries are caused by abuse by a third party. Circumstances may arise, however, in which one person is medically examined for another person's benefit. This may happen where a person is medically examined in order to gain employment. A negligent diagnosis or examination would have consequences for both the patient and the prospective employer.

The fulfilling of a statutory duty can give rise to a common law duty of care. This may happen in the context of a hospital accident and emergency service or an ambulance service, both of which operate on a statutory basis. A problem exists in so far as the pursuer may have suffered injury before the service took over their care, but the statutory duty brings the parties into a proximate relationship with one another. In the English case of *Kent* v *Griffiths* (2000) it was held that the duty arises in the case of an ambulance service when the call is accepted.

## STANDARD OF CARE

In all negligence actions the requisite standard of care is that of reasonableness. In medical negligence cases it is the same, with the important difference that the requisite "normal and usual" practice is assessed by expert evidence which itself must be reasonable. This is the case because of the specialised nature of medical practice and the fact that judges, lawyers and lay persons are not able to reach a decision as to reasonable care without recourse to medical evidence. The practice of medicine is also an art form rather than a pure science. As such, there is scope for different opinions of good medical practice. The requisite standard is that level of care exercised by the competent medical practitioner acting in the class of practitioners usually occupied by the defender practitioner. There are no "degrees of negligence", but a single standard of care that is to be applied to all circumstances.

## Historical development

The principle imputing wrongfulness from acting with a lack of skill in a professional capacity comes from the Roman law: *spondet peritiam artis, et imperitia culpae adnumeratur* translates as "he is responsible for skill in his profession, and want of such skill is regarded as a fault". That principle was cited with approval in *Gerrard* v *Royal Infirmary of Edinburgh NHS Trust* (2005), coming, as it did, half a century after the landmark judgment in *Hunter* v *Hanley* (1955). But before that, and until the early 20th century, the principle applied in the context of contract, as its application in the Roman law was in Aquilian liability in respect of damage to one's slave (Justinian), which amounted to damage to property as opposed to personal injury.

Reported cases of actions for medical negligence first appeared in the late 19th and very early 20th centuries. *Dickson* v *Hygienic Institute* (1910) dealt with the conduct of a dental practitioner. The court found that where a person holds themselves out as having a high degree of skill carrying out treatment under contract, the required degree of skill is that of other members of his profession.

It is this expectation of a high degree of skill that led to the apparent approval of a test for "gross negligence" as appropriate in cases of medical negligence. This position was settled in the watershed case of *Hunter* v *Hanley* in 1955, in which it was found that in civil liability for medical negligence there is no room for gross negligence. Indeed, there are no "degrees of negligence", but a single standard that must be applied to all medical claims.

### *The test in* Hunter v Hanley

In the benchmark case of *Hunter* v *Hanley* (1955), the plaintiff had received a series of intra-muscular injections of penicillin in her hip. The needle broke and remained embedded. Further surgery did not remove the needle. She sued on the ground that a doctor with an average knowledge ought to have known to use a stronger needle. This begged the question of what was the normal practice as to the type of needle to use. Lord President Clyde set out a general test: to succeed in a negligence action in medical negligence in diagnosis or treatment, it must be established that the doctor is guilty of a failure that no doctor of ordinary skill would make if acting with ordinary care.

The Lord President went on to note that deviation is not in itself evidence of negligence; if it was, it would impede medical progress and innovation. In deviation cases, he required three elements to be proven. These were that:

1. there is a usual and normal practice;
2. the defender did not adopt that practice; and
3. "the course the doctor adopted is one which no professional man of ordinary skill would have taken if he had been acting with ordinary care".

Crucially, it is insufficient to prove that the pursuer's injury is caused by the defender's deviation. It must be established that the deviation was negligent.

This tripartite test applies to *deviation* cases. If there is no usual practice, or if the usual practice was not followed, the more general test applies. This general test is the one set out above: that is, whether the doctor has been proven guilty of such failure as no doctor of ordinary skill would be guilty of if acting with ordinary care.

In England the test was set out in *Bolam* v *Friern Hospital Management Committee* (1957). In that case the plaintiff underwent electro-convulsive therapy for depression but was not given relaxant medication. He suffered fractures to his skull. His case in negligence alleged a negligent failure to give him the drugs, to restrain him and to warn him of the risks inherent in the procedure.

The evidence was to the effect that some practitioners would have given drugs or employed greater restraints in the absence of medication, while others would not have done so. The test in *Hunter* v *Hanley* was altered slightly and expressed as follows: "A doctor is not guilty of negligence if he acted in accordance with a practice accepted as proper by a responsible body of medical men skilled in that particular art." NcNair J argued that the difference was only a matter of expression, but that did not stop commentators arguing that there was a different test in Scotland from that in England and Wales. It was later held in *Maynard* v *West Midlands Regional Health Authority* (1985) that where a defendant acted in accordance with one of two opposing schools of practice, negligence could not be found.

The *Bolam* test was criticised as being determinative to the extent that the court simply approved medical expert opinion. But in *Bolitho v City and Hackney Health Authority* (1998), the House of Lords found that it is for the court to determine whether the body of medical opinion relied upon is itself reasonable. In that case the medical practitioner failed to attend and to intubate a 2-year-old boy with respiratory problems. It was found that he would not have died had the omission not taken place. The court found that despite a body of professional opinion sanctioning the defendant's conduct, the defendant may still be found liable. This is because the body of opinion relied upon must, in the court's opinion, be reasonable and responsible.

There has been considerable debate in both academic and judicial circles as to the differences between the tests in *Hunter v Hanley* and *Bolam/Bolitho*. Lord Caplan said in *Moyes v Lothian Health Board* (1990) that *Bolam* had "amplified" *Hunter*, but that in the end "the appropriate tests in medical negligence cases are to be found in *Hunter v Hanley* and *Bolam*". What is clear is that British courts will to some extent defer to the views of the medical profession.

## Normal or usual practice

As indicated above, where negligence is alleged, there may be a normal practice (which either was or was not adhered to) and there may not be such a normal practice.

Where it is alleged that the defender did not adhere to an established normal practice, the burden of proof on the pursuer will be considerable. However, once the deviation has been established, the burden shifts to the defender to justify that deviation. Although this is consistent with the law in England set out in *Clark v McLennan* (1983), it is inconsistent with the Scottish case of *Devaney v Glasgow Health Board* (1987). In *Devaney*, the pursuer had surgery to his aorta but suffered a cardiac arrest and paralysis after the operation. He argued that the surgeon had employed the incorrect technique. Although the evidence as to the risks involved was divided, the court found that the defender does not bear the onus of justifying the technique used. With the evidence split, it was not proven that the surgeon had acted in a way in which no other surgeon would have acted, and hence no negligence was found.

Following normal practice may still amount to negligence if, in the opinion of the court, the practice followed is found to be neither reasonable nor responsible. This follows the judgment in *Bolitho* in England. In the Scottish judgment of *Gordon v Wilson* (1992), the court found that where there are two bodies of conflicting but reasonable medical evidence, the court is powerless to prefer one over the other. The court can, however, prefer one professional interpretation of medical *facts* over another and can test credibility and reliability of expert witnesses.

In *Gordon* v *Wilson*, the pursuer alleged negligence in failing to diagnose a brain tumour at an early stage and sued in respect of the resultant nerve damage caused by the delay. Two experts were heard, to the effect that it was unusual for a general practitioner to encounter a brain tumour and that very few tumours were meningiomas, as was the case in the defender's instance. One expert felt that an urgent referral to a specialist should have been made, while the other felt it unjustified in the circumstance. Both experts were considered credible and reliable. Lord Penrose drew on the *Maynard* judgment to find that preference for one body of opinion was not enough to establish negligence. This stance has been upheld in *Beasley* v *Fife Health Board* (2001) and *Honisz* v *Lothian Health Board* (2006).

Several cases have left open the possibility in Scots law of the court rejecting expert evidence. For example, in *Phillips* v *Grampian Health Board* (1991), Lord Clyde found that evidence of a body of opinion opposing the pursuer's case will be fatal to that case unless it is entirely rejected by the court. And the judgment in *Bolitho* has been cited with approval in Scottish courts, although without holding that the evidence in question was in fact illogical or unreasonable. In *Duffy* v *Lanarkshire Health Board* (2001), the court found that decisions of medical professionals must be "capable of withstanding logical analysis, and be seen as reasonable and responsible".

The tripartite test for deviation cases as set out in *Hunter* v *Hanley* (1955) requires the establishment of a normal practice, but the general test caters for situations in which there is no normal practice. Yet there is case law to the effect that the tripartite test applies only where a deviation from normal practice is alleged, but that failure to establish that there is a usual practice (the first leg of the tripartite test) may not be fatal to the case. In such situations, the only question for answer will be whether the defender is guilty of a failure that no doctor of ordinary skill would make if acting with ordinary care. This was the case in *Gerrard* v *Royal Infirmary of Edinburgh NHS Trust* (2005).

## Medical risks and benefits

Of primary importance when the medical practitioner is making any calculation of medical risks and benefits that the practitioner must make is that their judgement will, in all facets of medical care, be subject to the test set out in *Hunter* v *Hanley* (1955). This includes whether a risk ought to have been taken, whether it should not have been taken; when it was taken; and whether a patient should have been informed of a risk inherent in the procedure.

The case law is clear that negligence will be found if a practitioner knowingly takes an easily avoidable risk. In *Hucks* v *Cole* (1993), the defendant failed to administer penicillin and septicaemia set in. Where, on the other hand, there is a high risk of the patient dying or their condition worsening, that factor may be weighed against the side-effects of the treatment. In *Duffy* v *Lanarkshire Health Board* (2001), the pursuer had had a bone marrow transplant to treat aplastic anaemia which she alleged she had contracted as a side-effect of the drug chloramphenicol. The Extra Division found that the doctor was not negligent in weighing the possible side-effects against the fatal nature of aplastic anaemia, as five different courses of antibiotics had not treated the pursuer's underlying pathology.

## Inexperience

A medical practitioner must act responsibly within their scope of experience, but inexperience is no excuse in a negligence action. The maxim *imperitia culpae adnumeratur* is applied, as discussed above. In *Steward* v *Greater Glasgow Health Board* (1976), the pursuer alleged negligence in failing to assess a mother's condition properly at the time of her daughter's birth, leading to brain injury to the daughter. Negligence was also alleged in the carrying out of the delivery by vacuum suction. The defenders were absolved because the practitioners had acted according to accepted practice in an emergency situation. But Lord Keith also said that negligence could be established where a practitioner failed to seek help when required and where circumstances allowed and where injury could have been avoided thereby.

In the English case of *Wilsher* v *Essex Area Health Authority* (1988), the court found that inexperience is no excuse. In that case the plaintiff suffered from several conditions caused by his prematurity, including oxygen deprivation. He went on to contract retrolental fibroplasia and consequent blindness caused by a catheter having been inserted into a vein rather than an artery, resulting in him receiving excess oxygen on two occasions. The defendant health authority argued that inexperience should result in a lower standard being applied to the conduct of the junior doctor in question. This argument was rejected by the court, which found that all medical staff must meet the standard of competence and experience expected of those holding such posts.

## Negligent treatment and errors of judgement

All areas of medical practice are subject to *Hunter* v *Hanley* (1955), but the main areas considered by the courts are diagnosis and treatment. Negligent treatment cases can arise in any medical scenario, including during and following childbirth. Negligence was found in *Hunter* v *Glasgow Corporation* (1971), for example, where midwives failed to remove the afterbirth completely, causing sepsis necessitating surgery. The exploratory operation was performed unskilfully, causing organ damage and necessitating a hysterectomy. Statistically speaking, however, most allegations fail to prove negligence.

The question arises whether errors of judgement can amount to negligence. According to the English case of *Whitehouse* v *Jordan* (1980), they can – although Lord Denning in the court below had initially argued that they did not. In that case, a senior hospital registrar attempted a forceps delivery. He pulled six times to no effect, as the child had become impacted, and a caesarean section was performed. However, the impaction had led to oxygen deprivation. The evidence turned on the professional judgement of whether the defender had "pulled too long and too hard" on the forceps, leading to the impaction. In the House of Lords' judgment, the court found that errors may or may not be negligent, depending on whether the error does or does not pass the test in *Bolam* in England and Wales or in *Hunter* v *Hanley* in Scotland.

*Whitehouse* was relied on in Scotland in *Phillips* v *Grampian Health Board* (1991) which found that it is not enough for a pursuer to establish an error of judgement; it must also be established that the error was one that no doctor of ordinary skill would make.

## Diagnosis

In *Moyes* v *Lothian Health Board* (1990) the patient underwent an angiography, which is a diagnostic procedure carrying a risk of stroke, which the patient suffered. In *Gordon* v *Wilson* (1992) (discussed above), the pursuer sued for the failure to diagnose a tumour earlier. In both cases – and in subsequent case law – it was held that the test in *Hunter* v *Hanley* applies to diagnosis as well as treatment. Further, if symptoms should cause a competent doctor to investigate further, failure to do so may amount to negligence. In *Johns* v *Greater Glasgow Health Board* (1989), the patient had a fall and went to hospital. Her swollen wrists were overlooked, hence an X-ray was not ordered and fractures were not diagnosed. Negligence was found.

## Emergencies

As indicated above, defenders must act according to accepted practice in an emergency situation (*Steward* v *Greater Glasgow Health Board* (1976)). This is also the position in England. In *Kent* v *Griffiths* (2000) it was held that in the case of an ambulance service, a duty arises when the call is accepted. In *Barnett* v *Chelsea and Kensington Hospital Management Committee* (1968), three night-watchmen became ill after drinking tea. They were taken to the casualty department where they were told to go to their own doctors. One of the men subsequently died of arsenic poisoning following a negligent failure by the casualty officer to examine him properly. However, while it was found that the *Bolam* standard applies to emergency situations as well as diagnosis and that by that standard the defendant was found negligent, the plaintiff failed to establish causation and so did not win the case.

## CAUSATION

The general rule is that negligence is said to have caused injury if, but for the negligence, the patient would not have suffered the injury. Conversely if – as was the case in *Barnett* v *Chelsea and Kensington Hospital Management Committee* (1968) involving arsenic poisoning – the injury would have occurred regardless of the proven negligence, causation is not established. This is the "but for" or *sine qua non* test. This test covers simple issues of cause and effect. However, in some circumstances several agents may contribute to the injury, in which case a test that establishes a material contribution will be required. In other cases, a pursuer may have been exposed to a harmful agent, in which case a test for a material increase in risk will be required.

Among other things, the judgment in *Fairchild* v *Glenhaven Funeral Services Ltd* (2002) looked at the extent to which causation is a question of fact. Lord Hoffmann found that it was, because rules of law set out particular requirements which determine the scope of liability (legal causation). The question of fact is whether the rules of liability have been satisfied (factual causation).

### The "but for" test

Generally, where a legal injury would *not* have occurred but for the negligence of the defender, causation will be established and the pursuer's case won. This must be established in both general and individual terms.

This may be a matter of medical fact, as was the case in *Kay's Tutor* v *Ayrshire and Arran Health Board* (1987). In that case it was established that a penicillin overdose – albeit negligently administered – does not, as a matter of fact, cause deafness. The deafness was caused by the child's underlying meningitis. Damages were, however, awarded for *solatium* – for the temporary suffering of the child as a result of the overdose.

A different facet of causation is exemplified in *Kenyon* v *Bell* (1953). That case indicated a more individualistic approach to the "but for" test, which takes into account the particular circumstances of the patient and their pathology. A child was injured in a car accident, receiving a cut to her eye. Her eye had to be removed. Despite proof of negligence, the court rejected the pursuer's claim, on the medical evidence that the particular patient would have lost her eye anyway.

## Material increase in risk

Arguably the strictness of the "but for" test has been relaxed by judicial acknowledgment of the sufficiency of material increase in risk as establishing causation. In the classic case of *McGhee* v *National Coal Board* (1973), the pursuer was employed in a brick works. No washing facilities were provided. He had to cycle home without showering first, and suffered dermatitis. It was found that the failure to provide washing facilities was negligent. The House of Lords found that there was no real difference between saying that the omission had led to a material increase in risk and saying that there had been a material contribution to that injury.

The *McGhee* judgment has served as authority in the medical negligence field. In the case of *Wilsher* v *Essex Area Health Authority* (1988) (discussed above in respect of the negligent administration of excess oxygen), the excess oxygen could have caused the blindness suffered, but the retrolental fibroplasia that led to the blindness could also have been caused by one of four other conditions from which the plaintiff already suffered (iatrogenic injury). The House of Lords held that, following a finding of negligence, the onus lay on the plaintiff to show that the negligence had caused the injury. The plaintiff had not discharged this burden.

*Fairchild* v *Glenhaven Funeral Services Ltd* (2002) was an industrial disease case involving the asbestos-related illness mesothelioma. The employers were negligent in not providing protection from inhaling asbestos dust. The House of Lords adopted a modified approach to causation that became known as the "*Fairchild* exception". This exception allows a departure from the "but for" test in material contribution cases. The court in *Fairchild* found that the court in the *McGhee* judgment had applied a less stringent "but for" test that equated material contribution with factual causation. The extent to which these judgments might apply to medical negligence cases remains unclear.

Even so, there is the suggestion in *McGhee* that because the defenders materially increased the risk of the pursuer contracting dermatitis, the onus shifted to the defender to show that whatever caused the illness, it was not the extra time required before the pursuer was able to wash the dust off his skin. Yet attempts in *Wilsher* and in *Craig* v *Glasgow Victoria and Leverndale Hospitals Board of Management* (1976) to use Lord Wilberforce's judgment in *McGhee* to shift the burden of proof in medical negligence cases were rejected by the court.

## Loss of chance and loss of opportunity

Correctly diagnosing a condition should lead to an outcome more favourable than incorrectly diagnosing the condition. The purpose of the civil law and the law of delict is to restore the pursuer to the position they would have been in but for the negligence. This leads to arguments on the loss of chance to make a complete recovery, because of negligent misdiagnosis. In *Hotson* v *East Berkshire Area Health Authority* (1987), the court found that it could not rule that in no circumstances could a plaintiff succeed by proving loss of chance of a complete recovery. In that case a 13-year-old boy fell out of a tree. The hospital failed to diagnose a fracture to his knee. A correct diagnosis was made 5 days later, by which time lack of blood supply had led to permanent disability. The defendant argued that the fall was the sole cause of injury. The plaintiff argued that the delayed diagnosis led to the loss of the chance of a complete recovery (there was a 25 per cent chance of a complete recovery had the correct diagnosis been made). The Court of Appeal awarded 25 per cent of the damages the boy would have received had he proven his case completely, but the House of Lords reversed this decision because the judge's decision amounted to a finding of fact which had not been established.

In Scotland it is not possible to claim for the loss of the chance for a better medical outcome. In *Kenyon* v *Bell* (1953), a 6-month-old girl was found lying on the kitchen floor, bleeding from a cut to her eye. The casualty doctor instructed a nurse only to put drops in the eye and to apply powder. The parents were told it would not be necessary to see their family doctor. It was later found that there was internal haemorrhaging to the eye as well as a detached retina, necessitating the removal of the eye. The pursuer's main argument was for the loss of the eye; failing that, the pursuer claimed loss of a material chance that the eye could be saved. The court found that unless there could be drawn a reasonable inference that the eye could have been saved had the defender exercised proper care, the claim must fail. Similarly, if the cause of losing the eye were uncertain, the pursuer's claim would fail.

Loss of chance of a better medical outcome is different to the "loss of opportunity" cases. Scottish courts have considered the "loss of opportunity" caused by misdiagnosis in cases in which, for example, there was the loss of the opportunity to terminate a pregnancy because of misdiagnosis of Down's Syndrome in the foetus. This was the case in *McLelland* v *Greater Glasgow Health Board* (1999). The defenders admitted negligence and the court had to rule on damages for *solatium* and for the cost of the child's care. Damages were implicitly awarded for loss of opportunity, because all heads of damages flowed from the finding that had the pursuer known that trisomy 21 existed, she would have terminated the pregnancy.

In the not dissimilar case of *Goorkani* v *Tayside Health Board* (1991), the pursuer succeeded in establishing negligence (albeit in treatment). Yet he failed to prove that had he known of the risk of sterility from taking a particular drug, he would not have taken the drug. He failed to discharge this burden of proof of causation because he would have gone blind without the drug. However, the court awarded him damages for *inter alia* loss of the opportunity to become accustomed to his pending infertility (see Chapter 5 on consent, for further discussion).

## Factual and legal causation

Legal causation considers those facts that should be used to establish causation and the use of causal language to do so. This may by way of the *sine qua non* ("but for") test, which is a test for the chain of causation between the negligence and the injury. That chain may be broken by an intervening act of a third party or the pursuer themselves, known as a *novus actus interveniens*. In such a circumstance, causation is not established. For example, in *McFarlane* v *Tayside Health Board* (2000), a child was born following a failed sterilisation operation the risks of which were not adequately explained to the pursuer. On policy grounds, the court found that the pursuer's failure to have an abortion or to give the child up for adoption could not constitute a *novus actus interveniens*. This is similar to the position taken in *Emeh* v *Kensington and Chelsea Area Health Authority* (1984).

However, a different position was taken in *Sabri-Tabrizi* v *Lothian Health Board* (1998) in which a failed sterilisation led to a pregnancy. The pursuer had an abortion but continued to have sexual intercourse with her husband, leading to a further pregnancy and delivery of a stillborn child. The House of Lords found that she should have known, following her pregnancy and abortion, that there remained a residual risk of pregnancy and that in the circumstances to have sexual intercourse without contraception constituted a *novus actus interveniens*.

For further discussion of the relationship between causation and the test for breach of the duty of care, see Chapter 5 on causation in information disclosure cases, in particular the judgment in *Chester* v *Afshar* (2004).

## DEFENCES

Defences to allegations of medical negligence may be either complete or partial. Complete defences include statutory limitation and partial defences include contributory negligence. In the former case, the defender is absolved, while in the latter case the award of damages is apportioned.

### Limitation

This is the most commonly invoked defence. It applies under the Part II of the Prescription and Limitation (Scotland) Act 1973. Under s 17, in actions for personal injuries, a claim must be brought within 3 years (the triennium) of the date when the injuries were sustained or, where there has been a continuing act or omission, within 3 years of the date on which the act or omission ceased, whichever is the later. A continuing act or omission may occur in drug prescription cases. For example, in *Kennedy* v *Steinberg* (1998) the pursuer alleged ongoing negligence in prescribing the depression medication Equanil, to which she had become addicted. The court found that the triennium ran from the date on which, in the opinion of the court, it would have been reasonably practicable for the pursuer in all the circumstances to be aware that:

1. the injuries were sufficiently serious to justify bringing an action of damages;
2. they were attributable to an act or omission; and
3. the defender was a person to whose act or omission they were attributable.

It is not sufficient for the pursuer to argue that they were not aware of the limitation period or that they failed to see a solicitor until after the triennium had expired.

Reasonable impracticality can be inferred from circumstances and is to be distinguished from reasonable excuse. Reasonable excuse amounts to averments such as those made in *Mackay* v *Lothian Health Board* (2001) in which the pursuer said that there was nothing to prompt him to question the defenders' conduct. Courts would not side with the pursuer in such circumstances. According to *Elliot* v *J and C Finney* (1989), a reasonable excuse for not raising the question is if gathering sufficient information on which to base the question would entail excessive time and money.

In *Phillips* v *Grampian Health Board* (1991), the pursuer was admitted to hospital in 1978, with a swollen testicle. No biopsy or surgical exploration was carried out. Although gonorrhoea was diagnosed, the medical report did not exclude tumour. More than a year later, the patient was referred to a urological unit and testicular cancer was diagnosed, with a secondary cancer in his lungs. Subsequent treatment proved unsuccessful; he died 7 years later, of lung failure. In the meantime, in 1985 he had commenced a negligence action, which was continued by his wife. The court found that it had been reasonably practicable for him to discover before July 1982 that his cancer was due to the delay and that the delay had been caused by the hospital's error.

Lord Clyde had observed in the *Phillips* case that, under s 19A of the 1973 Act, there is an unfettered judicial discretion to allow an action to be brought, notwithstanding the provisions in the Act. This discretion is exercised sparingly, sometimes after a preliminary proof on limitation. Where factors in favour and factors against prejudice to the pursuer in not allowing the claim are equally balanced, the court must refuse to exercise its discretion in favour of the pursuer. The weight attributed to each factor is determined by the Lord Ordinary and can be set aside by a higher court only if there has been an error of law.

Where the failure was due to the solicitor's negligent failure to bring the case within the triennium, the pursuer's action is against the solicitor rather than the medical practitioner (*Leith* v *Grampian University Hospital NHS Trust* (2005), citing *Forsyth* v *A F Stoddart & Co Ltd* (1985)). The same standard of professional negligence applies to solicitors as applies to medical practitioners, although the pursuer will bear a double burden: proof that the solicitor was negligent in failing to being the case in time and proof that had the claim been brought with in the triennium, the pursuer would have won that case. Otherwise the pursuer will have failed to prove causation in the case against the solicitor because, but for the solicitor's negligence, the outcome of the medical negligence case would have been unaffected.

## Illegality

From the maxim *ex turpi causa non oritur actio* (no action arises from immorality) comes a theoretically possible but rare defence against a medical negligence obligation. *Clunis* v *Camden and Islington Health Authority* (1997) concerned the obligation on the health authority to prevent the patient from committing a crime. Following the patient's discharge, several appointments were missed and the plaintiff committed manslaughter, to which charge he pleaded guilty. He argued that the health authority had been negligent in preventing him from committing the offence. The court would not let itself be used to enforce obligations arising from illegal acts.

## Therapeutic privilege

If a defender can prove that the patient would have suffered psychological disadvantage had the material information been given to him, the defence of therapeutic privilege would be established. This is discussed in Chapter 5 on consent.

## Contributory negligence

Where damage is suffered in part caused by the conduct of the pursuer, fault may be apportioned between the litigating parties under the Law Reform (Contributory Negligence) Act 1945. Although there are no cases in which a finding of contributory negligence has been made in English or Scots medical law, such a finding is theoretically possible. In *Farquhar* v *Murray* (1901), for example, the doctor went on leave for 9 days, leaving instructions for the patient to apply a poultice to his diseased finger. The patient failed to do so, necessitating an amputation. Although the pursuer failed to prove his case in negligence, the court observed that had the negligence been established, the case may have been one in which the patient might have been found to have contributed to his injury.

## ALTERNATIVES TO *CULPA*

The existing system is based on fault, but there are from time to time moves to reform it in order to speed up the process, reduce damages payouts and the cost of litigation and even redress the balance between pursuer and defender. Some areas of law and medicine have been reformed. The Consumer Protection Act 1987 governs pharmaceutical injury and is operative in the area of private law. The Vaccine Damage Payments Act

1979 provides payments for damage suffered as a result of State-sponsored vaccination programmes and operates in public law terms a statutory system of State liability.

## Products liability

Although the Consumer Protection Act 1987 protects the consumer, the purchaser of a drug has an arguably more effective remedy in the law of contract. This is because where a prescription is dispensed privately under a contract between pharmacist and patient, there is an implied term of the contract that the goods are of satisfactory quality. This remedy would not, however, be open to a patient on the National Health Service as there is no contract in existence.

In other circumstances, liability for injury by a pharmaceutical product may be in negligence or in contract under the product's warranty. A duty of care is owed to consumers by manufacturers of medicinal and other products. However, a system of strict liability was established by the Consumer Protection Act 1987, which was enacted under obligations flowing from the European Products Liability Directive and the Pearson Commission Report. It came into force on 1 March 1988. Its terms apply to the whole of the United Kingdom and are reserved to Westminster under Part 5 of the Scotland Act 1998.

Actions are often brought by a group of parties similarly injured by a medicinal product, including pharmaceutical products and medical devices (prostheses). Although the "class action" is not allowed in Scots law, group actions do occur, with several "lead cases" representing a group. This was the case in *A* v *National Blood Authority* (2001).

In bringing an action under the 1987 Act, a claimant must establish:

1. that the device or medicine in question falls within the definition of "product";
2. the identity of the "producer";
3. defect in the product; and
4. injury and causation.

The defender may be able to make use of the statutory "development risk" defence.

### Product and producer

Other than saying that the definition includes products comprised within other products (eg a pump on a dialysis machine), there is no definition of "product" in the Act. The Directive does, however, consider that all moveables fall within the definition. "Producer" is defined as the person who manufactured it, won or abstracted it (in the case of a substance that was not manufactured) or the person who carried out the process giving rise to the essential characteristics of the product (if it was neither produced nor won or abstracted, as would be the case for agricultural produce).

There has been speculation as to whether blood and blood products fall within this definition. Blood certainly falls within the definition of "substance" under ss 1 and 45 of the 1987 Act. Considered along with the definition of "producer", this would suggest that the blood transfusion authority would be considered the "producer" of blood "products".

The English case of *A v National Blood Authority* involved six lead cases in which claimants had contracted Hepatitis C from transfusions of blood or blood products. The question arose as to whether Factor VIII platelets constituted "products" under the 1987 Act. The court found that they did.

The defender is the person who stands to gain from the marketing of the product and the person who creates the risk. Producers are, for the most part, manufacturers, although suppliers can fall within the definition. In the Act, "producer" includes manufacturers, distributors, importers and the companies who brand the product. This definition includes the prescribing medical practitioner and pharmaceutical chemist, who should be able to identify the manufacturer in order to avoid liability.

### Defect

Under s 3 of the 1987 Act, the definition of "defect" is the failure to meet the standard that "persons generally are entitled to expect". This is a test very close to that of reasonableness in negligence, but is arguably tighter as it is about more than careless production, concentrating as it does on the quality of the product itself.

The 1987 Act contains a definition of "safety" and elaborates on what persons generally are entitled to expect. Safety is defined relative to the risk of personal injury or death and account should be taken of the "manner in which and the purposes for which the product has been marketed, its get-up, the use of any mark in relation to the product, or warnings with respect to, doing or refraining from doing anything in relation to the product". This may have to do with the labelling of the product, packaging that will not allow access to children, and so on.

In *A v National Blood Authority* the court referred to the Directive rather than the Act, but the definitions of safety and entitlement to expect are the same. It was found that persons generally are entitled to expect transfused blood to be infection-free.

## Causation

The onus is on the pursuer to prove causation of harm. The same rules existing in the law of negligence are to be applied under the Consumer Protection Act 1987. This may be a problematic matter of scientific fact, particularly if it is required to separate the damage occasioned by the medicinal product from the damage caused by the disease itself (iatrogenic injury). In *A* v *National Blood Authority* (2001) the court found that "the defect was the virus in the blood and the damage was the virus in the patient". The causal link was in the science.

## Prescription periods

The same triennium limitation period applies to actions under the 1987 Act as applies in cases of negligence. The consumer must being a claim within 3 years of it being reasonably practicable for him to do so. There is, however, a prescription period of 10 years. This means that the claim is extinguished 10 years after the "relevant period", being the supply of the product.

## The "development risk" and other defences

Also known as the "state of the art" defence, this applies where the state of scientific and technical knowledge among producers of similar products was not, at the time, such that the defect might be expected to be discovered. There is an arguable difference in the 1987 Act from that in the Directive in so far as reasonableness exists in the United Kingdom version. This was considered by the European Court of Justice in *European Commission* v *United Kingdom (re the Product Liability Directive)* (Case C–300/95) (1997). In that case the court found that the defence in the 1987 Act could be interpreted more broadly than that in the Directive, but that it had not been shown that the United Kingdom had gone against the spirit of the Directive.

There are various reasons why a defect may not be known or knowable, including economic feasibility of discovery of the defect. These are tested along similar lines to a negligence enquiry – that is, through the use of reasonableness. A defect may also be either foreseeable or indeed known, but remain undiscoverable in practice; for example, unsafe only in a minority of cases that clinical testing will not reveal. Limited scientific and technical knowledge may obscure the defect from being discovered. An often-cited example is that of the drug Thalidomide in the 1960s.

In *A* v *National Blood Authority* the defence was used, but the court found that the defence did not apply where the risk was, or ought to have been, known. Once a defect is identified, the defence cannot logically be used. This finding did not stop the court making an assessment of the state of scientific knowledge at the time.

While the partial defence of contributory negligence may apply, the 1987 Act sets out further defences, including compliance with existing European Community law, that the defender was not the supplier of the product or that certain facets of the claim are competently refuted.

## Vaccine damage

Because vaccine programmes are promoted by the State, the Pearson Commission recommended strict liability compensation. This led to the Vaccine Damage Payments Act 1979, although there is case law in *Ross* v *Secretary of State for Scotland* (1990) in which it was argued that in promoting vaccination the Secretary of State had exercised its discretionary power irresponsibly and was negligent in the way it promoted the programme. The court found that attacks on the use of ministerial discretion must show bad faith.

As well as the Pearson Commission recommendation, scenarios giving rise to cases such as *Loveday* v *Renton and Wellcome Foundation* (1990) led to the 1979 Act. *Loveday* dealt with brain damage following administration of the pertussis (whopping cough) vaccine, although the plaintiff failed to prove causation and did not win his case.

The 1979 Act applies to the following vaccines: diphtheria, tetanus, poliomyelitis, tuberculosis, measles, smallpox, whooping cough (pertussis), rubella, haemophilus Type B infection, meningococcal Group C and mumps. It provides lump-sum payments for death or severe disablement as a result of these vaccines. There is no need to prove fault or negligence. It is, however, necessary to establish causation, which is a considerable hurdle for claimants.

Under the Vaccine Damage Payments Act 1979 Statutory Sum Order 2000, this sum is up to £100,000. Claims are settled by the Department for Work and Pensions. If refused, there is a right of review by a tribunal constituted under the 1979 Act.

This area of law is devolved to the Scottish Parliament, yet, perhaps because the relevant departments in Scotland and in England consult with one another, statutory instruments are enacted on a national basis. The logic appears to be to ensure that the same regime exists north and south of the border.

## Blood products liability: HIV and hepatitis C

Over the years, various funds have been set up to compensate those who have contracted blood diseases through transfusions. The Macfarlane Trust was set up by the Haemophilia Society to administer government funds. *Ex gratia* payments of £20,000 were made to those infected, but not to partners. Family members of deceased patients also received payments. The Eileen Trust aimed to help non-haemophiliacs who also contracted HIV from blood products. It administers lump-sum settlements from Scottish Executive funds.

Following *A v National Blood Authority* (2001), the Scottish Executive decided to make payments along the lines of that judgment to patients in Scotland. However, claimants could not avail themselves of these terms because of when the Act came into force and the fact that liability prescribes within 10 years. An expert group was set up under Lord Ross, on the recommendation of the Health and Community Care Committee of the Scottish Parliament, which recommended that *ex gratia* payments be made to those who contracted hepatitis C through blood transfusions.

Under s 28 of the Smoking, Health and Social Care (Scotland) Act 2005, Scottish Ministers may establish a scheme for making payments by them to persons who before 1 September 1991:

1. were treated with blood transfusions (blood, tissue or blood products) anywhere in the United Kingdom under the NHS and who became infected with the hepatitis C virus and did not die before 29 August 2003.

2. were infected with hepatitis C by one of the people in the above category and did not die before 29 August 2003. This category of person includes spouses, civil partners, cohabitants and certain blood relatives.

The *Report of the Expert Group on Financial and Other Support* (the Ross Report) had a broader remit than hepatitis C. It was charged with considering from a wholly Scottish point of view, and making recommendations on the reform of the system of medical negligence, including the substantive law, procedure, legal aid, mediation, and access to justice, as well as the possible introduction of no-fault compensation or strict liability. Consideration of the Ross Report falls outwith the scope of this book.

## Essential Facts

*Liability*

- The basis of liability lies in delict rather than contract.
- Liability is seldom borne by the individual doctor, as his employer will usually be vicariously liable. Liability may, however, be joint and several.
- An indemnity scheme operates for doctors working in the National Health Service.

*The duty of care*

- A duty of care exists by virtue of the doctor–patient relationship in respect of acts or omissions made in the context of that relationship.
- The existence of a duty of care is based on the principles of proximity (between the parties) and foreseeability (of harm).
- The duty of care will not arise for "pure omissions", as no duty to rescue is imposed on a doctor in the absence of a doctor–patient relationship.

*The standard of care*

- The standard of care required of medical practitioners is set out in *Hunter* v *Hanley* (1955).
- Practitioners must attain the level of care of the reasonable medical practitioner in their field.
- The expert evidence relied upon to justify the case for either pursuer or defender must itself be reasonable and responsible.
- Where deviation from usual practice is alleged, the tripartite test must be established, ie that there is a usual practice, that the defender did not adopt that practice and that "the course the doctor adopted is one which no professional man of ordinary skill would have taken if he had been acting with ordinary care".
- It is for the court to determine whether the body of medical opinion relied upon is itself reasonable.
- The burden of establishing that the duty of care was breached is on the pursuer.
- All facets of medical practice are subject to the test in *Hunter* v *Hanley* (1955), including diagnosis, treatment and information disclosure.

- Inexperience is no excuse in a negligence action.
- Errors of judgement may amount to negligence.

*Causation*

- It is necessary for the pursuer to prove that the negligence caused the injury, which is a question of fact.
- Proof of causation is through the "but for" test; that is, proof that but for the negligence, the pursuer would not have suffered the injury complained of.
- Where there are several causal agents, material contribution to the injury may amount to causation in law.
- There is no action for loss of the chance of a better medical outcome, but there may be an action for the loss of the opportunity to mitigate or avoid the damage suffered.
- The chain of causation may be broken by a *novus actus interveniens*.

*Defences*

- Defences may be complete or partial.
- Other than *novus actus interveniens*, complete defences include disproving part of the pursuer's case; the 3-year statutory limitation period having expired; illegality; or therapeutic privilege.
- An example of a partial defence is contributory negligence, which will lead to apportionment of the damages award.

*Alternatives to* culpa

- There has been piecemeal reform of the fault-based system from time to time.
- Reforms have led to the Consumer Protection Act 1987 which deals with products liability.
- Under the 1987 Act there is a requirement to prove that the damage was caused by a product made by a "producer", as defined in the Act. There is a requirement to prove defect, but not fault.
- Under the 1979 Act there is no requirement to prove causation. It is an example of strict liability.
- The defender may have recourse to the "development risk" defence.
- Other instruments include the Vaccine Damage Payments Act 1979 and various *ex gratia* schemes relating to blood products liability and HIV or hepatitis C.

## Essential Cases

**Edgar v Lamont (1914):** the existence of a contract for medical treatment by a doctor does not bar an action in delict by the patient against the doctor, for personal injury arising from the treatment. A contract for medical or dental treatment raises a duty to take reasonable care the breach of which is negligence which founds an action based not on contract but on delict.

**Roe v Minister of Health (1954):** the standard of care in contract and in delict is the same: that is, based on reasonableness

**Bonthrone v Secretary of State for Scotland (1987):** vicarious liability can exist only in the context of a contract of employment. General medical practitioners are independent contractors whose actions will not be defended by the National Health Service or Secretary of State.

**Morrison v Forsyth (1995):** there is no duty on a doctor to rescue or attempt to rescue a person where the doctor–patient relationship has not already been established and where contact occurs in that context.

**Fairlie v Perth and Kinross Healthcare NHS Trust (2004):** in general, the duty of care is owed only to a doctor's patients.

**Kent v Griffiths (2000):** in the case of an ambulance service, a duty of care arises when the call is accepted.

**Hunter v Hanley (1955):** generally, a doctor is negligent if he has been proven guilty of such failure as no doctor of ordinary skill would be guilty of if acting with ordinary care, but the tripartite test applies to deviations from practice: that is, it must be established that there is a usual practice, that the defender did not follow it and that "the course the doctor adopted is one which no professional man of ordinary skill would have taken if he had been acting with ordinary care".

**Bolam v Friern Hospital Management Committee (1957):** "A doctor is not guilty of negligence if he acted in accordance with a practice accepted as proper by a responsible body of medical men skilled in that particular art."

**Maynard v West Midlands Regional Health Authority (1985):** where a defender acted in accordance with one of two opposing schools of practice, negligence cannot be found.

**Gordon v Wilson (1992)**: preference for one body of opinion over an equally credible body of opinion is insufficient to establish negligence. The test in *Hunter* v *Hanley* (1955) applies to diagnostic procedures as well as treatment.

**Bolitho v City and Hackney Health Authority (1998)**: it is for the court to determine whether the body of medical opinion relied upon is itself reasonable.

**Moyes v Lothian Health Board (1990)**: "the appropriate tests in medical negligence cases are to be found in *Hunter* v *Hanley* and *Bolam*".

**Devaney v Glasgow Health Board (1987)**: the onus of proof is on the pursuer, throughout.

**Phillips v Grampian Health Board (1991)**: evidence of a body of opinion opposing the pursuer's case will be fatal to that case unless it is entirely rejected by the court.

**Duffy v Lanarkshire Health Board (2001)**: decisions of medical professionals must be "capable of withstanding logical analysis, and be seen as reasonable and responsible".

**Hucks v Cole (1993; opinion delivered in 1968)**: negligence will be found if a practitioner knowingly takes an easily avoidable risk.

**Duffy v Lanarkshire Health Board (2001)**: life-threatening delay should be weighed against the risk of harmful side-effects of the proposed cure.

**Steward v Greater Glasgow Health Board (1976)**: acting in accordance with medical practice absolves the defender, but failure to seek help when required and where circumstances allow and injury could have been avoided thereby will amount to negligence.

**Wilsher v Essex Area Health Authority (1988)**: all medical staff must meet the standard of competence and experience expected of those holding such posts. The onus of establishing causation rests on the plaintiff.

**Whitehouse v Jordan (1980)**: errors of judgement can amount to negligence.

**Phillips v Grampian Health Board (1991)**: it is not enough for a pursuer to establish an error of judgement; it must also be established that the error was one that no doctor of ordinary skill would make.

**McLelland v Greater Glasgow Health Board (1999)**: damages may be awarded based on the loss of opportunity for a different outcome had diagnosis been made correctly.

**Fairchild v Glenhaven Funeral Services Ltd (2002)**: causation is a question of fact as to whether the rules of liability have been satisfied.

**Kay's Tutor v Ayrshire and Arran Health Board (1987)**: causation must be established as a matter of medical fact in general scientific terms.

**Kenyon v Bell (1953)**: causation must be established as a matter of medical fact as applied to the particular case. If the cause is uncertain, the pursuer's claim will fail even if there is a material chance that "but for" the negligence the injury would not have been suffered.

**Fairchild v Glenhaven Funeral Services Ltd (2003)**: causation is a question of fact. The "Fairchild exception" allowed a departure from the "but for" test in material contribution cases.

**McFarlane v Tayside Health Board (2000)**: a child was born following a failed sterilisation operation the risks of which were not adequately explained to the female pursuer. On policy grounds, the court found that the pursuers' failure to have an abortion or to give the child up for adoption could not constitute *novus actus interveniens.*

**Sabri-Tabrizi v Lothian Health Board (1998)**: continuing to have sexual intercourse without contraception constituted a *novus actus interveniens* where the pursuer knew there to be a residual risk of pregnancy.

**Kennedy v Steinberg (1998)**: the triennium runs from the date on which it is reasonably practicable for the pursuer to be aware that the injuries are sufficiently serious to justify bringing an action of damages; that they are attributable to an act or omission; and that the defender was a person to whose act or omission they were attributable

**Clunis v Camden and Islington Health Authority (1997)**: the court will not let itself be used to enforce obligations that arise from illegal acts.

**A v National Blood Authority (2001)**: Factor VIII blood platelets constitute "products" under the Consumer Protection Act 1987: "[T]he defect was the virus in the blood and the damage was the virus in the patient." The causal link was in the science. The development risk defence did not apply where the risk was, or ought to have been, known.

# 5 CONSENT

As regards the legally competent adult patient, actions in consent follow a pattern common to other common law countries and are litigated in negligence. There is a rebuttable presumption of competence in adults. Treatment without consent may be an assault (the English law of trespassory touching does not form part of Scots law). With consent being a defence to an action in assault, the onus is on the defender to establish that consent was given by the pursuer. Where this burden is discharged by evidence of consent in broad terms, it may yet be alleged that consent was imperfect. If so, the case will be litigated under the law of negligence where damages will be sought for injuries caused – in the legal sense – by the doctor's failure to obtain complete or "informed" consent.

This usually means the failure to warn of an inherent risk in the procedure, where the pursuer argues that had they been so warned, they would not have given their consent and would not have suffered the injury. Where Scots law differs is that a possible action for wounded feelings is built into the common law.

This area of law is based on the patient's right to self-determination within the law of delict, as well as within the European Convention on Human Rights. That the right of self-determination forms part of this area of Scots law was confirmed by Lord President Hope in *Law Hospital NHS Trust* v *Lord Advocate* (1996) in which he said that the right solves the problems of consent as far as the court is concerned. As he put it, "consent renders lawful that which would otherwise be unlawful". To that end, the defence of *volenti non fit iniuria* is applicable, as it means that a legal wrong is not done to someone who is willing and so voluntarily assumes the inherent risk.

By implication, it is for the patient to determine whether to take a particular risk. The right to consent carries with it a right to refuse treatment. The corollary of the right of the patient is the duty of the doctor. This implies a test for the duty of care which will, as suggested above, be subject to the test in *Hunter* v *Hanley* (1955): the duty to warn of inherent risks forms part of the doctor's duty of care. The failure to inform of a risk may constitute lack of reasonable care. The court in *Moyes* v *Lothian Health Board* (1990) saw it this way: "Recognition by the doctor of the adult patient's right to make decisions about the risks he incurs is essentially an aspect of the duty to take reasonable care for his safety . . .".

In the case of adults who lack legal capacity by virtue of their mental incapacity, medical treatment will be justified where it is necessary, such as where the patient is unconscious and hence lacks capacity to consent.

According to *Re F (mental patient: sterilisation)* (1990), the doctor may administer medical treatment where it is in the patient's best medical interests: that is, performed either to save his life or to improve his condition. The Scottish Law Commission has indicated that the decision would be followed in Scotland, even although the Court of Session has the option of appointing a tutor dative. Further provisions under the Adults with Incapacity (Scotland) Act 2000 and the Mental Health (Care and Treatment) (Scotland) Act 2003 apply to proxy decision-making by a guardian or welfare attorney with authority to act on the incapable adult's behalf.

Minors who lack capacity by virtue of their age are governed by the Children (Scotland) Act 1995, which confers on parents the general responsibility to safeguard their child's health and represent his interests in medical decision-making. Children reach capacity at the age of 16 in Scotland, but may be capable of medical decision-making before that age. So-called competent minors are governed by the Age of Legal Capacity (Scotland) Act 1991, which creates an exception to the general rule that children under 16 cannot validly consent to medical treatment on their own behalf. They may consent if, in the opinion of the medical practitioner treating them, they are capable of understanding the nature and possible consequences of the proposed treatment.

## ASSAULT AND THE DEFENCE OF CONSENT

### Assault

Unlike the English law of trespass to the person, in Scots law the intentional invasion of bodily integrity constitutes an *iniuria*, which is a form of liability in delict based on affront. There is English judicial authority in *Chatterton v Gerson* (1981) for the proposition that the tort of battery is appropriate where there has been no consent, but that the failure to disclose an inherent risk should be litigated in the law of negligence.

Scottish authority is for the most part confined to the institutional and textbook writers, but the sheriff court case of *Thomson v Devon* (1899) concurred with the position that treatment without consent constitutes an assault, where a prisoner was vaccinated without his consent. In the unreported case of *Craig v Glasgow Victoria and Leverndale Hospitals Board of Management* (1976), the Court of Session was faced with a case of a man who had consented to exploratory surgery to investigate a swelling thought to be a cyst and to "any operation the surgeon considers necessary". In the event, the surgeon found and removed a carotid body tumour, but during the surgery the patient was deprived of oxygen and suffered brain damage. He brought a civil action in negligence and in assault. On the assault allegation, the First Division considered "necessary" to include any operation the surgeon saw as necessary and rejected the further argument that permission was limited to the minor operation discussed before surgery. The case was distinguished from those in which a different operation is performed to correct a different condition from that originally complained of.

As pointed out above, Lord President Hope in *Law Hospital NHS Trust* v *Lord Advocate* (1996) said that "consent renders lawful that which would otherwise be unlawful" and, by extension, elides the possibility of an action in assault. This was supported in *Bonthrone* v *Secretary of State for Scotland* (1987) in the Court of Session, in which the Lord Ordinary observed *obiter* that information to be provided to a patient by a doctor is governed by the normal test of professional negligence in *Hunter* v *Hanley* (1955).

If the assault is proven, the onus shifts to the defender to establish justification, for example by establishing that consent was given (*volenti non fit iniuria*). This might be contrasted with the English law in which it has been held in *Freeman* v *Home Office* (1983) that the onus of proving lack of consent in a battery case lies with the plaintiff. This case has, however, been criticised for being inconsistent with other English authority.

## Voluntary assumption of risk

The defence of voluntary assumption of risk (*volenti non fit iniuria*) is narrow in both English tort law and the Scots law of delict in so far as consent can be inferred from conduct – for example, the offering of an arm for taking blood pressure. This is the case only where there has been no misrepresentation on the part of the medical practitioner because, as a rule, consent must be freely and genuinely given. There is authority in the criminal law in *Hussain* v *Houston* (1995) to the effect that, in the instant case, consent was for a proper medical examination rather than what amounted to the indecent assault of three women patients (who were suffering from complaints unconnected with their genitalia). It remains the case in the civil law that a medical practitioner may not diverge from the treatment to which the patient has agreed to submit.

As *volenti* is a defence to a charge of assault, the burden of proof lies with the defender. In *Winnik* v *Dick* (1984), it was held that where there is a duty of care, successfully proving the maxim (*volenti*) means that the pursuer accepted the risk of the defender's negligence. This will absolve the defender from the consequence. The risk must, according to *Sabri-Tabrizi* v *Lothian Health Board* (1998), be assumed before or at the same time as the negligent omission.

It has, however, been argued that the *volenti* defence has no proper place in liability for the omission to provide information on attendant risks to medical procedures. This is because, the argument runs, the patient does not consent to negligence. Yet it is important to see such matters in the context of the voluntary assumption of risk. This, in turn, depends on the patient having been given adequate information on which to have freely based their consent to assume the risk.

## Criminal responsibility

While consent in broad terms elides the possibility of an action in the nominate delict of assault, further provisions apply to the crime of assault. When the court was considering the appropriate test for medical negligence, Lord Russell noted in *Hunter* v *Hanley* (1955) that "gross negligence" would be required to denote the level of recklessness required for the criminal law to become involved. This indicated that a substantially higher standard would be required than that required of ordinary *culpa*. Negligence – as tested by the rules set out in Chapter 4 – is insufficient. Medical treatment is unlikely to comprise the level of attack necessary to the offence of the "real injury" of assault. The contact between doctor and patient would require to be of such an order that it could not be defined as "treatment". In *Hussain* v *Houston* (1995), discussed above, the doctor was convicted of indecent assault because the contact with his patients bore no relation to their actual medical complaints.

## NEGLIGENT FAILURE TO OBTAIN INFORMED CONSENT

The onus of establishing that there was a failure to disclose the risks of a medical procedure is borne by the pursuer. This is consistent with the law of damages in which the party bringing the case in negligence bears the burden of establishing the elements of the action as *damnum* or wrongfulness is a necessary element of proof. It is necessary to prove that the omission to provide particular information was wrongful and that the omission caused or materially contributed to the pursuer's injury. This would be established where the pursuer proves that the omission caused them to not refuse treatment and hence to suffer the risk inherent in the treatment of which warning was not, in fact, given.

## Standard of care and wrongfulness

That a duty of care exists between doctor and patient is seldom in doubt and has been considered in Chapter 4 along with the standard of care in negligence. As indicated above, in *Bonthrone v Secretary of State for Scotland* (1987) the Lord Ordinary had observed that information to be provided to a patient by a doctor is governed by the normal test of professional negligence set out in *Hunter v Hanley* (1955) (the *Bolam* test in England: established by *Bolam v Friern Hospital Management Committee* (1957)).

In information disclosure cases, the alleged negligence is not in the performance of the surgical or medical procedure, but in the omission to provide information on inherent risks that is material to the patient's decision whether or not to give their consent.

This means that the adequacy or not of medical information provided to the patient, on which consent was based, is assessed by the courts according to the medical professional standard. However, the debate has for many years been on the relative merits of that standard as contrasted with a standard based on more objective factors unique to the particular patient (see *Arndt v Smith* (1997)).

The doctrine of "informed consent" was developed in the United States; it migrated to Canada and Australia, but as a doctrine has not found success in United Kingdom jurisdictions. This is because it holds that the standard of care under informed consent is that of the reasonable patient in the particular patient's position.

English law, in *Sidaway v Bethlem Royal Hospital Board of Governors* (1985), found that the professional standard as set out in the *Bolam* judgment was appropriate to information disclosure cases. There has subsequently been a trend away from a wholly medical professional standard. For example, in *Bolitho v City and Hackney Health Authority* (1998), the court required the medical opinion to be logical and coherent, so diluting to an extent the *Bolam* test. Courts' tendency towards adopting a less deferential attitude to the medical profession in favour of patients' rights culminated in the decision in *Chester v Afshar* (2005). In that case the House of Lords began with the presumption that standards of information disclosure had become patient-centred.

There is less case law on the point in Scotland, but it does indicate a medical professional standard that could follow the same trend in England.

In *McLaughlin* v *Greater Glasgow Health Board* (1981), the sheriff court dealt with a case of failed sterilisation of a female patient. The pursuer admitted that she had been informed in broad terms, but alleged that she had not been informed of the full implications, in a manner sufficient on which to found her consent. She argued that *Hunter* v *Hanley* (1955) is applicable to the mechanics of the practice of medicine and that a different standard should be applied to information disclosure. The court held that there was nothing in the scope of professional duty that should not be assessed according to *Hunter* v *Hanley*.

The Court of Session considered the issue in *Moyes* v *Lothian Health Board* (1990), in which the patient had a stroke which was a known risk of an angiography diagnostic procedure. This risk was raised in the pursuer's case because of her history of migraine and her hypersensitivity to the contrast medium. There had been a failure to warn of this aggravated risk. The patient failed to prove a hypersensitivity to the contrast medium. She argued unsuccessfully that the test in *Hunter* had been amplified in *Bolam* and modified by *Sidaway* to the extent that a patient has a right to be informed of those risks that would alter their decision on whether or not to give consent. Even so, the judgment in *Moyes* did attempt to take a patient-oriented approach through reference to the adult patient's right of self-determination. However, the precedent of *Sidaway* (albeit in English law but heard by the House of Lords) meant that the matter should be assessed according to medical professional criteria. Although the decision in *Moyes* indicates a sympathy towards the patient's position, subsequent case law in Scotland has not moved in the direction of a patient-centric approach, as is the case in England.

## Causation

The finer points of factual and legal causation have been discussed in Chapter 4. As is the case with any claim in delict and negligence, it is necessary to prove that the legal wrong caused the pursuer's injury. In cases of consent based on information disclosure, there will have been a negligent omission to warn of a risk. The patient will have suffered that risk. To prove a causal link, the pursuer must prove that but for the defender's omission, they would not have suffered the injury. To do this, the pursuer would need to assert that if they had been given information on the risk – ie assuming that there had been no omission to provide that information – they would not have given their consent and hence not suffered the injury. It may, however, be sufficient that the pursuer is able to establish that they would not have undergone the procedure *at that time* or performed *by that defender*.

The court did not need to consider causation in *Moyes* v *Lothian Health Board* (1990), because the pursuer failed to establish negligence, although in *Goorkani* v *Tayside Health Board* (1991), the court did consider the test for causation. The pursuer had lost sight in one eye, through Behcet's disease. He had been treated with a drug to prevent blindness in the other eye. The drug carried with it the risk of infertility. It was held that failure to warn of the risk of infertility was negligent, but the pursuer failed to prove that – in weighing up blindness and infertility – he would have refused to take the prescribed medication. Interestingly, he was awarded £2,500 for loss of self-esteem, shock and anger at the discovery of his infertility and the shock the discovery brought to his marital relationship. (This is discussed further below.)

In the English case of *Chester* v *Afshar* (2005), the plaintiff was not warned of the risk of post-operative paralysis following elective surgery to her spine. This risk eventuated. Although she asserted that, with a warning, she would have sought advice on alternative procedures, the judge was unable to make a finding as to whether she would have consented or not. Even if she would have delayed surgery, the risk was a random one (1–2 per cent) and hence the defendant's negligence was not the legal cause of her injury.

Significantly, the court found that causation was to be assessed by reference to the doctor's duty. The injury was within the scope of the duty of information disclosure and was a result of the risk of which it was the doctor's duty to warn. The injury was therefore to be regarded as caused by the negligent omission. This was a departure from traditional causation principles as a matter of legal policy which indicated a move away from medical paternalism and towards patients' rights.

It is arguable that with the trend exemplified in *Chester* v *Afshar* being towards patients' rights, rights of personality should be included. This is supported by the fact that the court in *Moyes* found the position in Scottish information disclosure cases to be reflected in the judgment in *Sidaway*. By implication, one could argue that further legal developments might be reflected in Scotland. Indeed, although judicial *dicta* have not yet done so, professional guidelines issued by the Scottish Executive Health Department's *A Good Practice Guide on Consent for Health Professionals* (2005) do reflect this.

## Remedies

Ordinarily, in delict and the law of negligence, the award of damages should reflect the pursuer's position had the negligence not occurred.

Yet in information disclosure cases – and assuming that the pursuer established that had they known of the risk they would not have undergone the treatment – damages should restore the patient to their position had they undergone no treatment. Without the treatment they would have been unwell. Damages awards tend to not reflect that, but rather to reflect the loss occasioned by the invasion of privacy. On that point, consider the award in *Goorkani* v *Tayside Health Board* (1991), discussed above, which reflected this, even although the pursuer failed to prove causation.

Based on the so-called "nervous shock" cases in English law, damages for psychiatric injury would not be awarded in the absence of physical injury. In Scots law, however, there is authority in *Stevens* v *Yorkhill NHS Trust and South Glasgow University Hospital NHS Trust* (2006) that the action of *solatium* for wounded feelings caused by an affront to the right of personality lies in the *actio iniuriarum*. However, this case dealt with unauthorised removal of organs (see Chapter 7) where, under the *actio iniuriarum*, the defender's conduct requires to be intentional. It is a moot point whether the *actio* can be developed or extended to cover affront caused by negligence.

### The exception of therapeutic privilege

If a defender can prove that the patient would have suffered psychological disadvantage had the material information been given to him, the defence of therapeutic privilege would be established. In *McLaughlin* v *Greater Glasgow Health Board* (1981), the doctor had explained the sterilisation operation to the pursuer, but had – according to the pursuer – not given her sufficient explanation to enable her to reach a decision on undergoing the operation. The defenders admitted that, ordinarily, it would be good medical practice to advise a patient of the risk of failure and that continued use of contraception would be required, but in this case subjecting the patient to potential anxiety was not sound medical practice. The pursuer's case failed on the strength of the test in *Hunter* v *Hanley* (1955). Similarly, in *Moyes* v *Lothian Health Board* (1990), Lord Caplan observed that clinical judgement may be used to determine whether a patient will be sufficiently alarmed as to be put off the treatment, or whether the level of alarm may render the treatment itself to be ineffective.

That said, the law has moved on since the judgments in *McLaughlin* and *Moyes*, through cases such as *Chester* v *Afshar* (2005), discussed above. This means that paternalism is less and less acceptable and hence that recourse to therapeutic privilege is appropriate only in exceptional cases.

## LAWFUL TREATMENT OF ADULTS WITH INCAPACITY

In respect of those over the age of 16 years, there is in Scots law a rebuttable presumption of capacity. Where a person lacks capacity by virtue of their mental incapacity – permanently, by virtue of their mental health or temporarily, perhaps by virtue of unconsciousness – treatment may be authorised in certain circumstances. These include necessity and authorisation under the Adults with Incapacity (Scotland) Act 2000. In these circumstances the treatment must be in the patient's best interests.

### Common law provisions

#### Necessity

Circumstances of emergency or medical necessity justify treatment without consent. The clearest example is the unconscious patient brought into hospital by ambulance, although a patient may have given consent to one surgical procedure, but during that surgery another procedure is deemed necessary: *Craig* v *Glasgow Victoria and Leverndale Hospitals Board of Management* (1976). The requirements for treatment to be lawful are that it is required for the patient's survival, rather than being medically convenient, and that there is a reasonable chance that consent will be given by the reasonable patient in that patient's position.

The English law was set out in *Re F (mental patient: sterilisation)* (1990). Treatment is lawful if it is in the patient's best medical interests, being necessary to save their life, improve their condition or prevent deterioration of that condition. According to the Scottish Law Commission in *Mentally Disabled Adults* (Scot Law Com Discussion Paper No 94, 1991), the decision in *Re F* would be followed north of the border. Indeed, the test in *Re F* was used in *L* v *L's Curator ad Litem* (1997), as discussed below.

Powers granted to doctors under the Adults with Incapacity (Scotland) Act 2000 are without prejudice to any other law, which may be taken to refer *inter alia* to the doctrine of necessity. The statutory provisions exist in addition to rather than as an alternative to existing provisions, unless otherwise specified. It is likely, however, that recourse should be had first to the provisions of the 2000 Act and if no applicable provision can be found there, recourse can be had to the doctrine of necessity, but this has not yet come before the courts in Scotland.

## Negotiorum gestio

The institution has been defined in Vol 15, para 632 of the *Stair Memorial Encyclopaedia* as "the voluntary management by one person (the *negotiorum gestor*) of the affairs of another (the *dominus negotii*) without the consent or even the knowledge of the other". It has in other civilian and mixed legal systems been extended to cover consent to medical intervention, albeit in emergency situations. It has not yet been extended beyond cases of patrimonial interests in Scots law.

## Treatment under the Adults with Incapacity (Scotland) Act 2000

### Legal history

Prior to the 2000 Act, use was made of tutors dative and tutors-at-law, responsible for the personal welfare of patients incapable of giving consent because of their mental incapacity. *L* v *L's Curator ad Litem* (1997) involved a young woman who suffered from autism. The court appointed her mother (the petitioner) as a tutor dative with power to consent to her daughter's surgical sterilisation. The test in *Re F* was used, that is, the treatment had to be in the patient's best interests ie necessary to save their life, improve their condition or prevent deterioration of that condition. The power of the court to appoint tutors dative and tutors-at-law was abolished by the Adults with Incapacity (Scotland) Act 2000.

Under the now-repealed Mental Health (Scotland) Act 1984, mental health guardians could be appointed by a sheriff. These guardians were normally nominees of the local authority, who could require adults to attend for treatment. They could also require access to be given to doctors, mental health officers and others.

### Medical treatment and research

The Adults with Incapacity (Scotland) Act 2000 provides for a process by which decisions can be made on behalf of adults who lack legal capacity to make them on their own behalf, by virtue of their mental incapacity. The 2000 Act replaced tutors to adults over 16 years of age with a range of sheriff court guardianship and intervention orders. Part 5 of the 2000 Act gives authority to medical practitioners to treat or undertake research on incapable adults under certain circumstances. In this way, both the vulnerable adult and the medical practitioner are legally protected. There is also a code of practice under the Act, which does not have statutory authority but may be used as an example of good practice.

"Incapable" and "incapacity" are defined in s 1(6) as being "incapable of acting, making, communicating or understanding decisions or retaining the memory of decisions as mentioned in the Act, by reason of mental disorder or inability to communicate because of physical disability".

The general principles under s 1 of the Act applicable to an intervention are that:

1. it should achieve a benefit not otherwise achievable;

2. it is the least restrictive option;

3. account is taken of past and present expressed wishes and feelings as far as this is practicable; and

4. there is consultation with another specified person or persons, as far as is reasonable and practicable. Specified persons include "[a]ny guardian, continuing attorney, welfare attorney or manager of an establishment exercising functions under [the] Act".

Part 5 of the 2000 Act requires the involvement of a "proxy" in decision-making. Under the Code of Practice, a proxy means a "welfare attorney, person authorised under an intervention order or a welfare guardian with powers relating to the medical treatment in question".

Welfare attorneys appointed under Part 2 of the Act may authorise medical treatment but may not give proxy consent to certain forms of treatment for mental disorder or place the granter in a hospital for mental disorder against their will.

In some circumstances medical practitioners may require the consent of persons authorised by a welfare intervention order issued under Part 6 of the 2000 Act.

### Authority of the medical practitioner

Under s 47 of the Adults with Incapacity (Scotland) Act 2000, where a medical practitioner primarily responsible for the patient's care certifies that he is of the opinion that a patient is incapable of making a decision on their own behalf in relation to the treatment proposed, the doctor may do what is reasonable in the circumstances. This authority is in relation to medical treatment and must be to safeguard or promote the physical or mental health of the patient. It may be exercised by someone else appointed by the doctor primarily responsible for the patient's care. There is a prescribed form for the certificate of incapacity. It must specify the period during which the authority will exist. This can be for up to 1 year. It may be revoked if circumstances change.

This authority does not include or authorise the use of force or detention, unless immediately necessary and only for as long as it remains necessary. Neither does it allow actions inconsistent with an existing court decision.

## Authorisation of treatment

### The parens patriae *jurisdiction and proxy consent*

As *parens patriae*, the Court of Session may act as the legal guardian of children and incapable adults. As such, it may exercise a common law jurisdiction to protect the interests of those people. It was in that capacity that the court appointed tutors dative, until such tutors were abolished by the Adults with Incapacity (Scotland) Act 2000. Before that, in *Law Hospital NHS Trust* v *Lord Advocate* (1996), the court found that the scope of the jurisdiction was not defined and neither can it be. Despite its abolition by the 2000 Act, the jurisdiction remains important with regard to the withdrawal of life support and as a mechanism to cater for unforeseen circumstances not covered by legislation.

Section 50 of the Adults with Incapacity (Scotland) Act 2000 makes provision for medical treatment where a guardian or welfare attorney has been appointed. If authorised under an intervention order, that person or body may have powers in relation to medical treatment. In disagreements between the doctor with primary responsibility for the care of the patient, and the proxy, the doctor is to ask the Mental Welfare Commission to nominate a second doctor to give an opinion. Authority to treat will be given if the second doctor agrees with the first, having consulted with the proxy.

Any person with an interest in the patient's personal welfare may appeal the decision to the Court of Session. This applies to the decision of the first doctor and that of the second. Decisions on medical treatment, other than those made under s 50, may be appealed to a sheriff court by any person with an interest in the patient's welfare.

### Research

The only research permissible on adults legally incapable of giving their consent is research into cause, diagnosis, treatment or care of their incapacity or other treatment administered during their incapacity. Further conditions are set out in s 51 of the Adults with Incapacity (Scotland) Act 2000. They include that the research is likely to produce a real and direct benefit to the adult or – in exceptional circumstances – where it is likely to improve scientific understanding of the adult's incapacity.

## Treatment

Provisions for consent to medical treatment are made in both the Adults with Incapacity (Scotland) Act 2000 and the Mental Health (Care and Treatment) (Scotland) Act 2003. The latter creates a framework for support for adults with a mental health disorder, whether or not their legal capacity causes them to fall within the ambit of the 2000 Act. The 2003 Act provides for both voluntary and compulsory treatment.

While mental disorder is defined in both Acts as including mental illness, personality disorder and/or learning disability, there are some differences between the two provisions. For example, they differ in their definitions of "adult" and of "incapacity", with the 2000 Act including those unable to communicate, while the 2003 Act does not contain that inclusion.

Authority to treat an incapable adult requires a certificate of incapacity under the 2000 Act, although the certificate will not authorise the use of force or detention other than in cases of necessity. Neither will it cover specific treatments such as electro-convulsive therapy or hospitalisation against the adult's will. However, when the adult is formally detained under the 2003 Act, and assessed as requiring treatment, the treatment must be authorised under the 2003 Act rather than the 2000 Act. Even so, under s 36 of the 2003 Act, those detained under the emergency provisions cannot be treated on a compulsory basis. If consent is required, it should be given by the adult himself or through a certificate issued under the 2000 Act.

## MEDICAL TREATMENT OF CHILDREN

### Responsibility of parents

Parents have the responsibility of ensuring that their children receive appropriate medical treatment. This is governed by the Children (Scotland) Act 1995. Based on the right to consent to a "transaction" on the child's behalf, parents also have the right to consent or refuse treatment on their child's behalf, as long as decisions are taken in the interest of safeguarding the child's health and welfare. This right is that of both parents, as long as it has not been removed from one of them as part of a divorce or custody settlement. Failure to fulfil this responsibility could expose the parent to the scrutiny of and sanction by child protection bodies.

Under the Children (Scotland) Act 1995, the Court of Session or a sheriff may make a specific issue order requiring a parent to consent to treatment on the child's behalf if that treatment is in the child's best interests and the parent has withheld their consent. The Court of Session retains its *parens patriae* jurisdiction over the exercise of parental power.

## Capable children below the age of 16

### Consent

Courts in England and Wales take a different approach to competent minors than that taken in Scotland. For a start, in Scotland a person is regarded as an adult for medical decision-making purposes at the age of 16. In England, the age of full capacity is 18. The difference is in the age at which constraints are imposed when it comes to refusals of consent: 16 in Scotland and 18 in England and Wales. Even so, both jurisdictions recognise the child's growing autonomy below 16 by applying versions of the so-called "*Gillick*" test.

The court in *Gillick* v *West Norfolk and Wisbech Area Health Authority* (1986) found that a child under the age of 16 may consent to treatment in their best interests where they have sufficient maturity and intelligence to understand the nature and implications of the proposed treatment. This is about the child's welfare as well as their capacity.

In Scotland, the Age of Legal Capacity (Scotland) Act 1991 abolished pupillarity and stipulates that the child under 16 lacks capacity to enter into transactions. However s 2(4) of that Act also stipulates that a person under the age of 16 years has the capacity to consent on their own behalf to surgical, medical or dental procedures if, in the opinion of a qualified medical practitioner, they are capable of understanding the nature and possible consequences of the proposed treatment. This is about the child's capacity, without reference to their welfare.

On the face of it, the difference between the two is that in Scotland the doctor is not required to make an assessment of whether the treatment is in the child's best interests.

It is important to stress that the omission of "best interests" from the Scottish legislation is a *prima facie* exception. The rationale is that the child has legal capacity to consent irrespective of considerations of welfare. This was a policy decision by the Scottish Law Commission in its 1987 foundation report. That report concluded that the "welfare" test would be restrictive, unnecessary and logically incoherent with a scheme in which a child had been found sufficiently mature to give his own consent.

Where there is a disagreement between the mature minor and their parent on the matter of consent, a specific issue order under the Children (Scotland) Act 1995 would not be competent, as the parents lose the right of veto under the 1991 Act where the child has been assessed as competent by the medical practitioner.

## Refusal

Most commentators in Scotland are of the view that the power to consent carries with it the power to refuse treatment. Courts in England and Wales have taken a different view. It remains to be seen whether it will be followed north of the border when such cases come before the courts. The cross-border differences are worth arguing, but the courts in Scotland have not yet ruled on the matter. In any event, the child's legal representative may act only where the child cannot do so. Indeed, in *Houston, Applicant* (1996) the sheriff found it illogical that the capable minor's decision should be overridden by his parent. Further, the power of refusal is implied in s 90 of the Children (Scotland) Act 1995, which provides that a child's consent to a medical examination is required, even in the presence of a court order or a supervision requirement of a children's hearing authorising the medical examination.

---

### Essential Facts

*Competent adults*

- Treatment of a competent adult patient without their broad consent amounts to the delict of assault.
- There is a rebuttable presumption of competence.
- The omission to provide information sufficient on which to base the patient's consent will amount to negligence. This is governed by the normal test of professional negligence in *Hunter* v *Hanley* (1955).
- It must be established by the pursuer that but for the omission to provide the information, he would not have consented to the medical procedure and hence not have suffered the injury.
- The exception of therapeutic privilege may apply where provision of otherwise material information would cause the patient undue anxiety and compromise his treatment.

*Incompetent adults*

- Treatment of adult patients who lack capacity by virtue of their mental health may be authorised if it is in their best medical interests or is justified by necessity. This is governed by the Adults with Incapacity

(Scotland) Act 2000 and the Mental Health (Care and Treatment) (Scotland) Act 2003.

*Minors*

- Treatment of minors under the age of 16 is subject to the consent of those with parental authority. This is governed by the Children (Scotland) Act 1995.
- Minors under the age of 16 who are mature enough to understand the nature and implications of the treatment may consent or refuse treatment on their own behalf. This is governed by the Age of Legal Capacity (Scotland) Act 1991. A capable minor's decision cannot be overridden by his parent.
- Despite statutory provisions, courts retain a residual *parens patri*ae jurisdiction.

## Essential cases

**Moyes v Lothian Health Board (1990)**: the right of a patient to decide about the risks he takes is a part of the doctor's duty to take reasonable care.

**Law Hospital NHS Trust v Lord Advocate (1996)**: the patient's consent renders lawful that which would otherwise be unlawful.

**Re F (mental patient: sterilisation) (1990)**: the doctor may treat the mentally incompetent patient where it is in the patient's best medical interests.

**Chatterton v Gerson (1981)**: the tort of battery is appropriate where there has been no consent; failure to disclose an inherent risk should be litigated in negligence.

**Thomson v Devon (1899)**: treatment without consent constitutes an assault.

**Craig v Glasgow Victoria and Leverndale Hospitals Board of Management (1976)**: "necessary procedure" includes any operation the surgeon saw as necessary at the time of surgery; permission was not limited to the minor operation discussed before surgery.

**Bonthrone v Secretary of State for Scotland (1987)**: information to be provided to a patient by a doctor is governed by the normal test of professional negligence in *Hunter* v *Hanley* (1955).

**Hunter v Hanley (1955)**: the standard of care expected is that which the reasonable medical practitioner would adopt in a similar situation

**Hussain v Houston (1995)**: the doctor was convicted of indecent assault because the contact with his patients bore no relation to their actual medical complaints.

**Winnik v Dick (1984)**: where there is a duty of care, successfully proving *volenti non fit iniuria* means that the pursuer accepted the risk of the defender's negligence; this will absolve the defender from the consequence.

**Sabri-Tabrizi v Lothian Health Board (1998)**: risks must be assumed before or at the same time as the negligent omission.

**Sidaway v Bethlem Royal Hospital Board of Governors (1985)**: the professional standard as set out in the *Bolam* judgment was appropriate to information disclosure cases.

**Bolitho v City and Hackney Health Authority (1998)**: the court required the medical opinion to be logical and coherent, so diluting to an extent the *Bolam* test; that test is applicable to the causation enquiry.

**Chester v Afshar (2005)**: the House of Lords began with the presumption that standards of information disclosure had become patient-centred. Causation is to be assessed by reference to the doctor's duty, as it is a duty to inform of a risk, which failure led to the risk materialising.

**McLaughlin v Greater Glasgow Health Board (1981)**: there is nothing in the scope of professional duty that should not be assessed according to *Hunter* v *Hanley* (1955). On therapeutic privilege: subjecting the patient to potential anxiety may not be sound medical practice.

**Goorkani v Tayside Health Board (1991)**: even if the pursuer fails to prove causation, having proved negligence, the court may award damages for *solatium*.

**Stevens v Yorkhill NHS Trust and South Glasgow University Hospital NHS Trust (2006)**: the action of *solatium* for wounded feelings caused by an affront to the right of personality lies in the *actio iniuriarum*.

**L v L's Curator ad Litem (1997)**: the test in *Re F* was used. Treatment must be in the patient's best interests, ie necessary to save his life, improve his condition or prevent deterioration of that condition.

**Gillick v West Norfolk and Wisbech Area Health Authority (1986):** a child under the age of 16 may consent to treatment in their best interests where they have sufficient maturity and intelligence to understand the nature and implications of the proposed treatment.

**Houston, Applicant (1996):** it is illogical that the capable minor's decision should be overridden by his parent.

# 6 CONFIDENTIALITY AND PRIVACY

The ethical standard of confidentiality dates back at least as far as the Hippocratic Oath, which specifies that all information gained in professional practice should be kept secret. In this clause lies the context of the doctor–patient relationship, as well as the obligation. The obligation has been part of Scots law for more than 150 years. Its breach entitles the victim to damages for *solatium*, as well as possible pecuniary remedies.

Although, in medical law, "confidentiality" is a term used in a broad sense that includes privacy, strictly speaking, in law there is a difference between privacy and confidentiality. Something is confidential once it has been confided in another party in the context of a relationship in which the obligation arises. Breach of the right to privacy comprises an intrusion into a private sphere.

Codes of practice have been published for the benefit of medical practice. Breach of these codes will serve only as evidence in support of the delict of breach of confidence in civil law. There is, however, statutory provision, in the Data Protection Act 1998 and the European Convention on Human Rights, that gives further definition to the right to privacy.

However, the duty of confidentiality is not an absolute. As we shall see, it exists subject to several exceptions such as breach justified in the public interest or by virtue of legal processes.

## MEDICAL PROFESSIONAL STANDARDS

The World Medical Association elaborated on the Hippocratic Oath in its Declaration of Geneva in 1947 to provide for respect for patients' secrets, even after their death. The declaration advocates a right of patients to expect this. If confidentiality were not presumed, the risk is that patients may be less forthcoming in consultation, to the detriment of their care. Yet the declaration anticipates that certain exceptions will apply.

In the context of the National Health Service in Scotland, the Caldicott Framework was introduced in 1999 to cater for a system in which it will not be the medical practitioner who handles the confidential information, but clerical and administrative staff.

## THE CALDICOTT FRAMEWORK

In 1999 the NHS in Scotland adopted, through a Management Executive Letter, the Caldicott Framework for England and Wales following the Caldicott Committee Report of 1997. That Framework recognised that the NHS is increasingly sophisticated and requires the transfer of patient data. It recommended the principles to be followed to ensure that patient-identifiable information is passed among government agencies only under certain conditions. It also recommended the introduction of guardians to ensure that an NHS number is used instead of the patient's name, for example. Any flow of patient-identifiable information should be tested against the following principles:

1. the use or transfer of information should be justified;
2. patient-identifiable information should not be used unless necessary;
3. the minimum necessary patient-identifiable information should be used;
4. access to patient-identifiable information should be on a "need to know" basis;
5. everyone on the clinical and non-clinical staff should be aware of their responsibilities;
6. every use of patient-identifiable information must be lawful.

The Security Advisory Group for Scotland (CSAGS) was set up and in 2002 published its *Final Report on Protecting Patient Confidentiality*. The report recommended against legislation giving statutory force to the exceptions to the duty of confidentiality as had been enacted in England and Wales. There has, however, been published an NHSiS *Code of Practice on Protecting Patient Confidentiality*. Scottish Ministers have also issued guidance in the form of the publication *Code of Practice on Confidentiality and Disclosure of Information*. The guidance is provided to contractors who provide services under the three NHSiS primary medical services contracts (general practitioners, for the most part).

## DOMESTIC AND EUROPEAN LEGISLATION

Although guidelines do not have statutory force, some provisions do exist, giving legislative force to the obligation of confidentiality in certain circumstances. This may have to do with the disease condition, as in the National Health Service (Venereal Diseases) Regulations 1974, or it may impose a more general duty of confidentiality on providers of primary medical services, as in the National Health Service (General Medical Services Contracts) (Scotland) Regulations 2004. For the most part, however, the duty is a common law one, albeit a duty considered in terms of the European Convention on Human Rights (ECHR).

Article 8 of the ECHR provides:

"1. Everyone has the right to respect for his private and family life, his home and his correspondence.

2. There shall be no interference by a public authority with the exercise of this right except such as is in accordance with the law and is necessary in a democratic society in the interests of national security, public safety or the economic well-being of the country, for the prevention of disorder or crime, for the protection of health or morals, or for the protection of the rights and freedoms of others."

Although there may be some conflict with Art 10 on freedom of speech as regards privacy, Art 8 has built into it some of the exceptions to the general rule. The European Court of Human Rights ruled on Art 8 and medical information in *Z* v *Finland* (1997). The court noted that respect for confidentiality was vital for public confidence in the health service and for the privacy of the patient. If there has been an apparent breach of confidence, it is important for the court to examine carefully the reasons for the disclosure. A three-stage test was set out by the court in order for disclosure to be justified. Disclosure must be:

1. in accordance with the law;

2. in pursuance of a legitimate aim (eg public interest); and

3. "necessary to a democratic society", which later case law found supported exchange of information among government agencies.

Domestic judicial interpretation of privacy and confidentiality under the ECHR is the concern of the common law.

## COMMON LAW PROVISIONS

Because Scottish case law on medical confidentiality is sparse, recourse might be had to the English law, which has in turn had recourse to Art 8 of the ECHR. Scotland is in effect a signatory to the ECHR as a component of the United Kingdom. Art 8 asserts the right to privacy.

The "equitable wrong" of breach of confidence in English law influenced the Scots delict of breach of confidence. Under both systems, the confider imparts information to the confident where unauthorised disclosure will allow a remedy.

This also applies to third parties who received the information knowing its nature to be confidential. In *X* v *British Broadcasting Corp* (2005), the Court of Session found that knowledge of the confidential nature of the information is to be tested subjectively rather than objectively. In addition, unless the disclosure is defamatory, there is no authority beyond *obiter dicta* for whether an action lies against a third-party disclosure that is *bona fide* or accidental.

## The tort of breach of confidence

In the English law, the classic formulation on breach of confidence was set out in the trade secrets case of *Coco* v *A N Clark (Engineers) Ltd* (1968). For an action to succeed, the information must be of a confidential character, disclosed in circumstances giving rise to an obligation of confidence and have been used without authorisation to the detriment of the confider. This was reformulated by both the *Spycatcher* case and by the ECHR.

In the *Spycatcher* case (*Attorney-General* v *Guardian Newspapers Ltd (No 2)* (1990), the House of Lords developed the equitable wrong of breach of confidence. It found that the duty arises when the information comes to the knowledge of the confider, where the confidant knew or agreed that the information was confidential. The place of this *dictum* in Scots law has been doubted in *Quilty* v *Windsor* (1999), arguably because it turned breach of confidence into a privacy tort.

In the *Spycatcher* case it was also stressed that the relationship between the parties could give rise to a duty of confidence and that the confident was bound (in equity) by conscience. While the relationship between the parties is important in Scots law, the delict of breach of confidence cannot be based on equity, which does not form part of Scots law.

The final requirement in the *Coco* test of harm to the confider is no longer required in English law (see *Cornelius* v *De Taranto* (2001), discussed below) and Scots law does not require harm other than wounded feelings (also discussed below).

In the *Spycatcher* judgment Lord Goff limited the duty of confidentiality. He found that once the information has entered the public domain, it is no longer confidential in nature. Neither does the duty apply to useless or trivial information. His third limiting factor was public interest: the public interest in disclosure may outweigh the general public interest in maintaining confidentiality. It is this balance which was struck between the right to respect for private life and the right to freedom of expression in Arts 8 and 10 respectively of the ECHR.

## Article 8 ECHR

The English law was further developed through the ECHR and s 6 of the Human Rights Act 1998, which comprises the transposition into domestic law of Art 8 of the Convention. In *Campbell* v *MGN Ltd* (2004), the House of Lords found that "the privacy of personal information [is] something worthy of protection in its own right". Medical information would fall within the definition of personal information in terms of the Data Protection Act 1998, for example. Article 8 and s 6 apply to Scotland.

In *von Hannover* v *Germany* (2005), the European Court of Human Rights found that under Art 8 of the ECHR, Member States are under an obligation to protect individuals from interference in their private life from public authorities. States must also ensure protection of private life between and among individuals. The domestic interpretation of the dictum in *von Hannover* came in *Douglas* v *Hello! Ltd* (2005) in which it was held that the State is under an obligation to protect individuals from invasion of their privacy by others. (That case concerned the publication of photographs of Michael Douglas and his wife Catherine Zeta-Jones by *Hello!* magazine, against their will and their having already sold the rights to the pictures to *OK!* magazine.)

There is some debate as to whether the effect of Art 8 should be a direct one in the domestic law or whether it should be an "indirect horizontal" one – that is, Art 8 should be given expression through the law of delict in Scotland or equitable wrongs in England. While the importance of Art 8 is stressed by the courts, there remains a tendency to resort to breach of confidence as the cause of action rather than using Art 8 directly as the cause of action.

## Invasion of privacy and breach of confidence

The "right to privacy" is understood to be the right to protection of personal information. This is different from confidentiality. Some information is inherently private. Once it is divulged in confidence, it becomes confidential too. This will be the case within the doctor–patient relationship. An action for breach of confidence, therefore, will not necessarily protect all private information. This is because some private information will already be in the public domain and hence not subject to confidentiality, yet still worthy of protection under Art 8. This was the case in *Douglas* v *Hello! Ltd* (2005), in which it was found that non-consensual photography of an individual in a public place could amount to an invasion of privacy. It would not, however, amount to a breach of confidence, although unfortunately in that case, the court had to "shoehorn" the invasion of privacy into an action for breach of confidence.

This begs the question of what information is "confidential" and what information is "private". In English law the judgment in *Attorney-General* v *Guardian Newspapers Ltd (No 2)* (1990) was developed in *A* v *B plc* (2002). The latter case found that a duty of confidence arises when a party subject to the duty "knows or ought to know that the other person can reasonably expect his privacy to be protected". In *Campbell* v *MGN Ltd* (2004), the court found that this also applies to the balancing of Arts 8 and 10 (privacy balanced against free speech). The duty of confidentiality arises when the publisher knows or ought to know that there is a reasonable expectation of confidence.

Significantly, there is no requirement for there to have been a prior confidential relationship. In *Douglas* v *Hello! Ltd* (2005), it was found that the nature and form of the information may be sufficient for the obligation to arise.

Certain types of information are recognised as confidential, such as medical information within the doctor–patient relationship. There are limits to considering medical information inherently confidential, however. According to the Court of Appeal in *Campbell* v *MGN Ltd* (2004), information on medical treatment is not the same as information regarding attendance at Narcotics Anonymous in the case of Naomi Campbell. The House of Lords, however, found that for there to have been a breach of confidence, the information disclosed must be private in nature and be information the claimant wants to protect. Because Naomi Campbell's treatment for drug addiction was about her physical and mental health, and her treatment, information about those matters was similar in nature to private and confidential information. It was therefore worthy of protection, as the assurance of confidentiality was essential to effective treatment.

### Striking a balance between privacy and freedom of expression

In *Campbell*, the court said that once information is deemed private, a balance should be struck between the individual's right to privacy and the public interest in publicity. These rights are reflected in Arts 8 and 10 of the ECHR, respectively. It is important to consider various facets of this balancing act and the provisions that will allow or prevent disclosure of otherwise private information.

## Freedom of expression

In *Reynolds* v *Times Newspapers* (2001), Lord Steyn considered freedom of expression to be the rule rather than the exception, with interference requiring justification. However, in balancing Arts 8 and 10, freedom of expression is not given any prior weighting. This is despite the fact that Art 10 includes the freedom to "receive and impart information and ideas without interference by public authority and regardless of frontiers". Article 10 does, however, specify that the right carries with it responsibilities and duties, with Art 10(2) providing for "preventing the disclosure of information received in confidence".

## Risk to third parties and detriment

Breach of confidence may be justified where there is a risk of harm to third parties or in the public interest. This is reflected in the General Medical Council guidelines on patient confidentiality, as well as in the case law. The scenario envisaged by this exception is one in which a crime may be prevented by disclosure. The GMC argues that patient consent to disclosure should ideally be sought.

In the English case of *W* v *Egdell* (1990), a psychiatric patient (W) who had been convicted of five manslaughter charges sought a transfer to a less secure facility. This required a medical report, which was produced by Dr Egdell. The report was unfavourable, contending that W remained dangerous and psychopathic. For this reason, the report was withdrawn by W's solicitor. Dr Egdell, however, passed his report on to W's hospital and W sued for breach of confidence. The court held that two public interests should be balanced against one another: the interest in confidentiality against the public interest in public safety.

In this case the interest in public safety prevailed, but the court found that disclosure has limitations. For example, it cannot be to the press or widely disseminated, but channelled to the correct public authority. It is also important that the risk is a real one.

The case of *Coco*, discussed above, required the element of harm to the party whose information is disclosed, in order for their claim in breach of confidence to be successful. It is difficult to envisage what harm might have been suffered by W had the court found the disclosure unjustified. Whether detriment to the complainant was required in medical confidentiality cases was settled in *Cornelius* v *De Taranto* (2001). In that case the disclosure itself was considered detrimental to the claimant even although the use of the disclosed report did not cause the claimant any other detriment.

This is not dissimilar to the position in Scots law in which an action would lie in *solatium* for wounded feelings arising from disclosure of private information. This would not require proof of patrimonial loss, as was the case in *AB* v *CD* (1904); *sub nom Watson* v *McEwan* (1905).

### HIV positive health care workers

The issue of HIV positive health care workers challenges the balance between the public interest in confidentiality against public interest in disclosure. In *X* v *Y* (1988) the court had to consider whether a newspaper was entitled to publish the names of two doctors with AIDS. Although, under the National Health Service (Venereal Diseases) Regulations 1974, the health authority must take steps to ensure confidentiality, the newspaper argued that disclosure was justified in the public interest. On the grounds that AIDS patients should feel uninhibited in attending for treatment and that the risk of transmission was negligible, an injunction preventing publication was granted.

### Unauthorised disclosure

There is some debate as regards the proper place for the cause of action in English law, where a confidence is breached. Traditionally regarded as an equitable wrong, there has been argument that the action should be in tort or in unjust enrichment (in the case of invasions of privacy through commercial publication, for example). What is clear in both English and Scots law is that courts are required to give effect to both Art 8 and Art 10 of the ECHR. This was made clear in *Douglas* v *Hello! Ltd* (2005). The court also found that it was unsatisfactory to "shoe-horn" privacy actions into breach of confidence even although it is arguable that Art 8 acts to separate the two actions.

### The actio iniuriarum and disclosure of medical records

In Scots law, breach of confidence is a delict, and courts are required to give effect to Art 8 on privacy. Yet it is unclear what direction the law is likely to take in this area. It is possible that Scots law could develop along similar lines to English law, using existing delictual categories or developing new categories. There is also authority for arguing that an action may lie in *solatium* for hurt feelings or affront under the *actio iniuriarum* This would be a comfortable fit, given the ruling in *Stevens* v *Yorkhill NHS Trust and South Glasgow University Hospital NHS Trust* (2006) and other case law. *Stevens* was discussed in Chapter 5. The court found that the action of *solatium* for wounded feelings caused by an affront to the right of personality lies in the *actio iniuriarum*. However, this case dealt with unauthorised removal of organs rather than a breach of medical confidence or invasion of privacy.

Yet the *action iniuriarum* sets out to protect rights of personality or *dignitas*, and includes protection of autonomy, privacy and confidentiality. It is also able to co-exist with the nominate delicts, including breach of confidence. For these reasons, it is arguable that Scots law will, when the time comes to rule on the matter, find little difficulty in accommodating Art 8 of the ECHR within the civilian tradition, because the *actio* is a rights based action that requires to balance competing rights, such as may be required between Arts 8 and 10. Courts would, however, still be required to apply the ECHR.

### Action against third parties

While *Lord Advocate* v *Scotsman Publications Ltd* (1989) did not determine when the obligation of confidence arises, neither a contract between doctor and patient, nor the existence of the doctor–patient relationship, gives rise to the obligation. This is a *prima facie* obligation. It is an implied term of the contract, where there is one, or a consequence of the legal relationship between doctor and patient, where there is not (see *AB* v *CD* (1904), discussed above). The question arises as to when the obligation can be imposed on third parties outwith the doctor–patient relationship.

Where confidential information is passed to a third party in breach of confidence, this does not mean that the information is in the public domain and hence that the duty of confidence falls away. There is still an obligation on the third party to keep the information confidential. In *Lord Advocate* v *Scotsman Publications Ltd* the court found this to be the case where the information was known by the third party to be confidential in nature and was received from a source other than the confider.

It was an open question as to whether the obligation applied to third parties who received the information without knowing it to be confidential. In its 1984 Report on *Breach of Confidence*, the Scottish Law Commission pointed out that one of the situations in which an obligation of confidence arises in respect of a third party is where a reasonable person in the circumstances would have realised that the information was confidential in nature. This may be due to the circumstances of disclosure of the nature of the information, such as medical records. In *Quilty* v *Windsor* (1999), the court found the action against a third party to be irrelevant in the absence of evidence that the documents in question had been transmitted in confidence by the hospital authorities, or were obtained by the defender in the knowledge that they had been communicated to him in breach of an obligation of confidence. There is support for this position in *Osborne* v *British Broadcasting Corp* (2000). As for cause of action, once again, the *action iniuriarum* may be appropriate as it arises from an affront following unauthorised disclosure of private information.

In *X* v *British Broadcasting Corp* (2005), the 17-year-old pursuer had agreed to be filmed in a television documentary about criminal court proceedings. She then withdrew her consent, seeking reduction of the "contributor's agreement" she had signed and an interdict against broadcast of the film. The defender argued that the information was in the public domain, as the actions that were filmed had taken place in a public place and material in a social services report read out in an open court. The court, however, found that the balance of Arts 8 and 10 fell in the pursuer's favour, as the personally important information was not readily available or in the public domain. This may appear odd, as the interdict was granted for breach of confidence, yet Art 8 is about a right to privacy.

The *actio iniuriarum* was invoked following unauthorised disclosure of medical records by a third party in *Russo* v *Hardey* (1997). The pursuer was a party litigant and disclosure arose during litigation. The general practice had sent records of both mother and son to the solicitor acting for the mother. On realising the error, the records were demanded back. They were sent back but the copies made were retained and used. The son alleged that the solicitors had wrongly used his records, albeit having obtained them by mistake. Proof before answer was allowed. It was found that the law recognises a duty of confidentiality on third parties and that the duty was a delictual one which could found an action for *solatium* alone.

## EXCEPTIONS TO THE GENERAL RULE

It was pointed out earlier in this chapter that, as well as a balance having to be struck between privacy and freedom of expression, the duty of confidentiality is not without exceptions. These are discussed below and range from express consent of the patient to justification in the public interest

### The health care team

Although clinical data should not be processed without the consent of the patient, their consent may be explicit or implicit. On confidentiality, the General Medical Council acknowledges the role that implied consent plays in what would otherwise be a breach of confidence, through the sharing of personal data among members of the health care team. This is necessary in the interests of the patient's care but, according to the GMC booklet on confidentiality, the doctor is required to ensure that the patient is aware that his information will be shared with other health care professionals engaged in that patient's care. This may involve professionals in the organisation primarily involved in the patient's care or information shared among various organisations, as may be the case if the patient is referred to a specialist unit. If the patient objects, this should be respected except if that will pose a risk to others and to the general public. In any event, it is important that where information is passed to other health care professionals, this is done on the understanding that it is confidential in nature.

## Clinical audit and express consent

The same principles applying to the health care team also apply to clinical audit, which is necessary in the provision of health services. Again, it is important that the patient is made aware that his personal information will be used in clinical audit and that he consents to that use. The information should be anonymised where possible and practicable but, where this is not possible or practicable, express consent should be given to the use of that data in clinical audit.

Express consent is also required for the disclosure of personally identifiable data used in research and administration. But once data is anonymised, it is no longer considered confidential, according to *R v Department of Health, ex parte Source Informatics Ltd* (2000).

## Legal processes requiring disclosure

In some instances the law will require disclosure of personal medical information. For example, some statutes expressly require notification of certain diseases and an action brought following personal injury would almost necessarily require disclosure of the nature of that personal injury.

### Legislation

The most obvious examples of statute not just allowing but compelling disclosure of medical information are the Infectious Diseases (Notification) Act 1889 and the Public Health (Scotland) Act 1897, as amended, which require disclosure by medical professionals to local authorities of cases of certain "notifiable" diseases: cholera, plague, relapsing fever, smallpox and typhus, and other diseases in "epidemic proportions". The name, age and sex of the patient are to be notified. Similar provisions apply under the Misuse of Drugs (Supply to Addicts) Regulations 1997, and the Abortion (Scotland) Regulations 1991.

In addition, there are statutes that require the provision of certain information to government bodies. For example, under regulations subordinate to the Medical Act 1983 and the National Health Service (General Medical Services Contracts) (Scotland) Regulations 2004, medical practitioners are required to maintain records pertaining to patient care and to provide certain information to health boards when required to do so. This exception may therefore be seen in the light of that concerning information passed among members of the health care team.

Under the Scottish Public Services Ombudsman Act 2002, where the Ombudsman is investigating a health service body – as one of the "listed authorities" falling within its purview – it may require listed authorities to supply information or produce documents relevant to the investigation, including patient records. Patient consent should first be sought for disclosure of identifiable information, although the GMC recognises that in some circumstances disclosure without consent may be justified, such as under the public interest exception.

## Litigation

Under both the common law and the Administration of Justice (Scotland) Act 1972, disclosure of personal data is justified for the purpose of enabling litigants to prove their averments in civil proceedings. This may be necessary in both criminal (assault) and personal injury litigation. Even so, objections may be raised on the ground of confidentiality or indeed public interest immunity. For example, in *P* v *Tayside Regional Council* (1989), a foster mother contended that she had contracted hepatitis B from a child placed in her care by a local authority. She applied for disclosure of the child's hospital records. The court rejected the defender's claim to public interest immunity on the ground that the public interest in justice outweighed that in confidentiality and that it would require a weighty public interest to prevent a party from litigating in favour of disclosure.

Although the information exchanged between doctor and patient is privileged, this does not exempt the medical practitioner from being required to give evidence in litigation. This is settled practice in the law of evidence and applies to both criminal and civil hearings, and is required to be considered in light of Art 10 of the ECHR.

## The *incapax*

Discussion of breach of confidence and the patient's consent begs questions surrounding the position of incapable adults and capable minors. In general, similar principles apply to these persons that apply in consent generally, as discussed in Chapter 5.

### Minors under the age of 16

As a general principle, both children and adults have a right to confidentiality, which includes information on medical matters as well as information held by carers and social workers. This takes on particular importance when it comes to competent minors and information kept confidential to the exclusion of their parents. While there are some similarities, the test for whether the competent minor is entitled to confidentiality is not the same as that applied to consent of competent minors.

A minor may wish that information on contraception or abortion be kept confidential. The court would not find this problematic where that minor has attained sufficient capacity under the Age of Legal Capacity (Scotland) Act 1991. Where, on the other hand, the minor has not met the test of competence under the 1991 Act, he would not have had the capacity to enter into that confidential relationship in the first place. In this instance the obligation of confidentiality would be in place only in exceptional circumstances and disclosure should be only to an appropriate third party, such as an advocate or carer.

(The right of confidentiality between spouses exists even in the instance of an abortion, because there is no right of veto under the Abortion Act 1967.)

### Incapable adults

Although the GMC advice is the same for incapable adults and minors, the Adults with Incapacity (Scotland) Act 2000 allows the medical practitioner primarily responsible for the patient's care some specific authority. This includes an authority to do what is reasonable in the treatment of the incapable adult, where "treatment" is broadly defined as "any procedure or treatment designed to safeguard or promote physical or mental health". Disclosure is therefore justified if it is in the patient's best medical interests. Refusal may require an appropriate certificate of incapacity, although consent may, under the 2000 Act, be given by the patient's proxy.

## Specific categories

Particular provisions as to disclosure of otherwise confidential information apply to specific categories of person. These categories include possible victims of abuse or neglect, the deceased patient and genetic information that may also apply to parties other than the patient. These are often around questions of confidentiality within the family.

### Victims of abuse

Where a doctor is aware of or suspects abuse or neglect by a family member, the GMC advises that the doctor must pass on this information to an appropriate authority or responsible person. This is done in the patient's best interests, but where it is felt disclosure would not be in the patient's best interests this should be discussed with an experienced colleague. This right to report is not a duty to do so, although the GMC advises that the police or social workers should be contacted.

### The deceased patient

Confidentiality should be maintained even after the patient's death. However, the obligation is flexible and depends on circumstances, including any directions from the patient before their death. Under the Access to Health Records Act 1990, their personal representative is allowed access to the health records of the deceased made after 1991, as is anyone who may have a claim arising out of their death. Relatives and successors may fall within this category.

### Genetic information

Because genetic information may apply to a patient's relatives too, the issue is a complex one. Several genetic conditions, such as cystic fibrosis, fall into the category of information which may be of interest to the patient's family, as disclosure may affect their decisions as to raising a family themselves or to have embryos screened before implantation. In such situations, a balance should be struck between the patient's interest in confidentiality and the public interest in limited disclosure, where family members are also members of the public.

### Anonymised data

In *R v Department of Health, ex parte Source Informatics Ltd* (2000), the applicant was a company which collected data on prescribing habits of general practitioners and sold this on to pharmaceutical companies. The data was anonymised first, by removing patient-identifiable data such as name, address and postcode. The Department of Health issued guidance to the effect that disclosure amounted to a breach of confidence. The company sought a declaration that the policy was wrong. The court held that disclosure was not a breach of confidence provided that the patients were not identifiable. As long as the patients' autonomy was not compromised and their privacy not put at risk, they had no property in the information or right to control its use.

## A duty to breach confidence

It has been considered whether, on the basis of some American jurisprudence, a situation could arise in which there is a duty to breach confidence in some circumstances. The American jurisprudence arose from the case of *Tarasoff* v *Regents of University of California* (1976). In that case, a university medical centre was found liable for not warning a woman that her former boyfriend had expressed violent feelings towards her during therapy. He went on to kill her and he was convicted of first-degree murder in *People* v *Poddar* (1973).

According to what became known as the "*Tarasoff* doctrine", there is a duty on a third party to breach confidentiality where the patient poses a threat to the third party who is the foreseeable victim of violence. The doctrine has been developed subsequently to apply to damage to property in *Hedlund* v *Orange County* (1983); to general unspecific victims in *Lipari* v *Sears* (1980); and to arson in *Peck* v *Counselling Service of Addison County* (1985).

It is considered that such a slippery slope would not be permitted in Scots or English jurisprudence because the doctrine, through its development, dispensed with the requirement of foreseeability, which is a strict requirement in tort and delict. For the wrong of a party to be actionable, a duty of care must first exist. In the scenarios of the American jurisprudence, foreseeability and proximity were insufficient to give rise to a duty of care in Scots law. This is clear from the line of nervous shock cases such as *Alcock* v *Chief Constable of South Yorkshire Police* (1992). *Tarasoff* was considered by the Bench in *Palmer* v *Tees Health Authority* (1999). It was found that in cases of harm to third parties, for liability to arise in negligence, an identifiable class of victim should exist, yet the question was left open regarding the position where the victim himself was in fact identifiable or identified

## REMEDIES

Disciplinary action by the General Medical Council should not be underestimated, as the consequences to the medical practitioner's career may be serious. Yet that can not be considered a remedy open to the patient whose confidence has been breached. Although there are several options open to the patient, none will be able to undo the wrong, as is the case in medical negligence more generally.

## Interdict

A patient may apply for an interdict where he is aware of imminent disclosure. This is a commonly sought remedy, but is of little or no use after disclosure.

## Delivery or destruction

Because medical records are owned by the NHSiS, they cannot be vindicated by the patient or their delivery demanded. They may be destroyed where they are incorrect or false, however.

## Financial damages

This remedy may be available where, for example, the patient suffered nervous shock that was foreseeable as a consequence of the breach of confidence. However, according to *Levin* v *Caledonian Produce Holdings Ltd* (1975) (a non-medical case) the measure of damages is the market value, which would not be high in the case of ordinary patients, but may be high in the case of celebrities.

## Damages for *solatium*

There may be grounds for an award of *solatium* for wounded feelings following unauthorised disclosure. There is justification for this in the judgment in *AB* v *CD* (1904), discussed above, as the Scottish Law Commission found that to be authority for disclosure causing wounded feelings to be a justifiable head of damages. In *Hardey* v *Russel and Aitken* (2003) the *actio iniuriarum* was invoked as a remedy for wounded feelings arising from the unauthorised disclosure of NHSiS medical records relating to the pursuer.

## Recompense

Where the defender has been unjustifiably enriched through the disclosure of confidential information, a remedy for recompense may be open to the pursuer. There is a justification for this in *Levin* v *Caledonian Produce Holdings Ltd* (1975).

## ACCESS TO MEDICAL RECORDS

Medical practitioners are required by regulations to maintain records of patient examinations and to ensure that those records are accurate and accessible. Patients, on the other hand, have certain rights of access to those medical records. These rights exist by virtue of several directives and conventions, such as the European Convention on Human Rights and Biomedicine. They also exist by virtue of domestic statute, from the Data Protection Act 1984 to the Access to Medical Reports Act 1988, the Access to Health Records Act 1990 and latterly the Data Protection Act 1998. Rights of access may also be allowed by virtue of the common law. While the records themselves are owned by the NHS or the general practice, the patient retains the right of access to the information in the records and may obtain a copy upon payment of a fee.

### The common law

Common law access may be justified by virtue of the litigation process discussed above as a reason for breach of confidence. It appears, however, that there is a rebuttable presumption against a right of access. *Boyle* v *Glasgow Royal Infirmary and Associated Hospitals* (1969) involved an action in damages raised by a couple following the death of their daughter. Their argument was that the mother had a right of access by virtue of having been a patient at the hospital. This argument was rejected, as the value of the records was in advancing medical science as well as in the interests of the patient's care. It was not in patients' best interest to allow access as of right. It is certainly arguable that the position has moved on since that case, particularly by virtue of statute.

### The Data Protection Act 1998

EC Directive 95/461 on the processing of personal data was implemented in the United Kingdom by the Data Protection Act 1998. Its subject-matter is reserved to Westminster under Sch 5 to the Scotland Act 1998. It has the aim of protecting privacy. Before the 1998 Act, access was governed by the statutes mentioned above. It repealed and replaced their provisions and came into force on 1 March 2000.

### *The eight data protection principles*

There are eight data protection principles and several data protection terms that were introduced by the 1998 Act. Section 1 indicates that the term applies to medical records. "Data" is information processed automatically or as part of a relevant filing system. "Personal data" is any data which identifies a living individual, including opinions on that person that may have been expressed by the doctor or health authority as "data controllers". For definition terms, medical data under the 1998 Act amounts to "sensitive personal data", being data about a person's mental or physical health or condition. Particular provisions apply to such data. According to the English case of *Durant* v *Financial Services Authority* (2003), to fit within the definition of "personal data", the data must not simply be capable of identifying the individual, but must impact on the data subject's privacy or have the subject as the focus of the data. In addition, the "filing system" in question must be of a high standard (using a system of cataloguing and indexing, for example). If the persons or the data involved do not fall within the definitions in the Act, the Act will not apply.

Data controllers (the practice or health authority) must, in the processing of sensitive personal data, adhere to the following eight principles:

1. Personal data must be processed fairly and lawfully, for example processing for medical purposes by a medical professional under an obligation of confidentiality and all that that implies.

2. Personal data must be obtained only for one or more specified and lawful purposes and may be processed only in ways compatible with those purposes. Under this principle, transfer of data to a third party, as discussed above, will require the explicit consent of the data subject and for the data controller to specify this purpose at the outset.

3. Personal data such as medical records must be adequate, relevant and not excessive in relation to the purpose or purposes for which they are processed.

4. Data must be accurate and kept up to date.

5. Data must not be kept for longer than is necessary for their purpose.

6. Personal data must be processed in accordance with the rights of data subjects under the 1998 Act, which specifies the *only* circumstances in which a person contravenes this principle.

7. Data controllers must take measures to prevent unauthorised processing or unlawful access to or destruction of personal data.

8. Personal data may not be transferred to a country or territory outside the European Economic Area unless that place ensures adequate protection in the processing of personal data.

## Access rights and exemptions

Section 7 of the 1998 Act gives patients rights of access to obtain copies of their personal data. The data must be communicated in an intelligible and permanent form, except where supply in a permanent form is impossible, would involve "disproportionate effort" or where the subject agrees. There is also a right of access to information on the source of the data. "Intelligible form" includes an explanation of terms and abbreviations and interpretation of slides and X-ray films.

Requests for data must be in writing, are required to be met within 40 days and may attract a prescribed fee. The data subject may request the entire record or only relevant parts. A second request for the same data may be made only after a prescribed period has passed, although account should be taken of the nature of the data and the frequency with which the data was updated.

The right of access is subject to certain exemptions. The Secretary of State may create such exemptions and has done so in the case of the Data Protection (Subjects Access Modification) (Health) Order 2000, which allows an exemption where access to the sensitive personal data would be likely to cause serious harm to the physical or mental health of the data subject or a third party. A further example applies to the Human Fertilisation and Embryology Act 1990. Access may be refused where another individual may be identified through that access, unless that individual has given their consent. This will not preclude provision of that data in an anonymised form which does not identify that individual. A court may be required to determine the reasonableness of this course of action. Account should be taken of the duty of confidentiality, steps taken to obtain consent and the person's capacity to give it, and whether there was an express refusal by that person. The possibility that disclosure may cause harm to the individual should also be taken into account.

## Third party rights

According to s 55 of the 1998 Act, third parties must not knowingly or recklessly obtain or attempt to obtain access to another person's personal data without the data controller's consent. This protects both the patient as data subject and the doctor as data controller. The exemption of necessity applies where, for example, disclosure is necessary for the prevention of a crime. Similarly, a public interest exemption applies. A person who reasonably presumes entitlement to access is also exempt from the prohibition. Contravention is an offence, as is selling the data or offering it for sale.

*Remedies*

Certain remedies for improper processing of data exist. These map on to those for breach of confidence discussed above.

Under s 13 of the Data Protection Act 1998, a person whose data is processed by the data controller contrary to the Act is entitled to compensation if they suffer damage or distress thereby. This may occur where processing of sensitive personal data is done that is not done in the interest of the data subject. Breaches envisaged in the Act are where processing is done for "journalistic, artistic or literary" purposes. With this in mind, damages may be on a compensation basis for the value of the data or on a *solatium* basis following distress caused by improper processing.

In addition, if the data is inaccurate, the subject may apply for an order for its "rectification, blocking, erasure and destruction". Application is to either the sheriff court or the Court of Session. This is in keeping with the eight principles set out above. The court would order rectification or replacement and destruction of the inaccurate record, or simply the addition to the record of a statement correcting the data.

## FREEDOM OF INFORMATION

Confidentiality and freedom of information are two sides of the same coin. The Freedom of Information (Scotland) Act 2002 grants a right of access to all types of information held by Scottish public authorities. This right is subject to exemptions, such as the information being confidential in nature. The Act also imposes certain obligations on public authorities, which includes all health bodies under the National Health Service in Scotland (NHSiS) umbrella.

Access is allowed to information that public authorities are under an obligation to disclose, unless it was obtained by the public authority under an obligation of confidentiality. Being two sides of the same coin, there is no obligation to divulge information that is the subject of the Data Protection Act 1998, although difficulties may arise as to which data falls within which category. These may need to be resolved by the Information Commissioner and may in turn be appealed to the Court of Session.

## Essential Facts

*Medical professional standards*

- The duty of confidentiality dates from the Hippocratic Oath and the Declaration of Geneva and has been given effect in the common law.
- The standards of the medical profession have been set out in guidance published by the General Medical Council.
- Scottish Ministers have also published guidance on confidentiality in the medical profession.
- Guidelines do not have statutory force.
- The duty of confidentiality is a common law one, but must be considered in terms of the European Convention on Human Rights.

*Domestic legislation and the ECHR*

- Article 8 of the Convention provides that everyone has the right to respect for their private and family life, home and correspondence. This may not be interfered with by a public authority other than in accordance with the law.
- Article 10 may be in tension with Art, 8 as it concerns freedom of expression.
- For disclosure of confidential information to be justified, it must be in accordance with the law, in pursuance of a legitimate aim and "necessary to a democratic society".

*Common law provisions*

- Scotland is in effect a signatory to the ECHR as a component of the United Kingdom. It is for the Scottish courts to determine matters relative to the Convention.
- Under English law, breach of confidence is an equitable wrong.
- Under Scots law, breach of confidence is a nominate delict.
- The tort of breach of confidence was set out in a line of cases leading to *Attorney-General v Guardian Newspapers Ltd (No 2)*, which found that the duty of confidence arises when the information comes to the knowledge of the confider, where the confidant knew or agreed that the information was confidential. The relationship between the parties could give rise to a duty of confidence. The confident was bound (in equity) by conscience.

- The requirement of harm to the confider is no longer required.

- The English law was further developed through the ECHR and s 6 of the Human Rights Act 1998, which comprises the transposition into domestic law of Art 8 of the Convention. In *Campbell* v *MGN Ltd* (2004) the House of Lords found that "the privacy of personal information [is] something worthy of protection in its own right".

- While the relationship between the parties is important in Scots law, the delict of breach of confidence cannot be based on equity, which does not form part of Scots law.

- Pursuers in Scotland may have a remedy through the *action iniuriarum*, which protects personality rights (*dignitas*) against invasion through the action of *solatium* for wounded feelings caused by the affront of invasion of privacy.

- *Douglas* v *Hello! Ltd* (2005) held that the State is under an obligation to protect individuals from invasion of their privacy by others under Art 8.

- The "right to privacy" is different from confidentiality. A balance requires to be struck between privacy and freedom of expression. Some information is inherently private. Once it is divulged in confidence, the recipient is bound by an obligation of confidentiality. Certain types of information are recognised as confidential, such as medical information within the doctor–patient relationship.

*Exceptions to the general rule*

- Breach of confidence may be justified by freedom of information, risk to third parties, the public interest and public safety, disclosure among members of the health care team, the data having been anonymised, clinical audit and express consent, and legal processes requiring disclosure (legislation and litigation).

- Similar principles that apply to the *incapax* and the capable minor in the law on capacity and consent, apply to those persons in relation to confidentiality.

- Provisions as to disclosure of otherwise confidential information apply to specific categories of person including possible victims of abuse or neglect, the deceased patient and genetic information that may also apply to parties other than the patient.

- The American *Tarasoff* doctrine (requiring breaches of confidence in certain circumstances) does not apply in Scots law.

*Remedies*

- Disciplinary action by the General Medical Council should not be underestimated, as the consequences to the medical practitioner's career may be serious.
- Further remedies include: interdict; delivery or destruction; financial damages; damages for *solatium*; and recompense.

*Access to medical records*

- Medical practitioners are required by regulations to maintain records of patient examinations and to ensure that those records are accurate and accessible.
- Patients have certain rights as regards access to their medical records by virtue of the eight principles of the Data Protection Act 1998. Section 7 of the 1998 Act gives patients rights to access and obtain copies of their personal data, which must be communicated in an intelligible and permanent form, except where supply in a permanent form is impossible, would involve "disproportionate effort" or where the subject agrees.
- The right of access is subject to certain exemptions such as public interest.
- Third party rights of access are not permitted, according to s 55 of the Data Protection 1998.
- Certain remedies for improper processing of data exist. These map on to those for breach of confidence.

*Freedom of information*

- The Freedom of Information (Scotland) Act 2002 grants a right of access to all types of information held by Scottish public authorities, subject to exemptions such as the information being confidential in nature.

### Essential Cases

**Z v Finland (1997)**: breach of confidence is justified if disclosure is in accordance with the law, in pursuance of a legitimate aim and necessary to a democratic society.

**X v British Broadcasting Corp (2005)**: third-party knowledge of the confidential nature of the information is to be tested subjectively rather than objectively.

**Campbell v MGN Ltd (2004)**: "the privacy of personal information [is] something worthy of protection in its own right." Medical information would fall within the definition of personal information; this can include information on treatment for drug addiction as it relates to physical and mental health. The duty of confidentiality arises when the publisher knows or ought to know that there is a reasonable expectation of confidence. This test can be used to balance of Arts 8 and 10 (privacy against free speech) of the ECHR.

**Douglas v Hello! Ltd (2005)**: the State is under an obligation to protect individuals from invasion of their privacy by others. There is no need for a prior relationship of confidence for the obligation to arise; the nature and form of the information may be sufficient.

**Reynolds v Times Newspapers (2001)**: freedom of expression is the rule rather than the exception; interference requires justification.

**W v Egdell (1990)**: public interest in confidentiality must be balanced against public interest in safety to justify disclosure of otherwise confidential information.

**Cornelius v De Taranto (2001)**: disclosure itself was considered detrimental to the claimant, even although the use of the disclosed report did not cause the claimant any detriment.

**AB v CD (1904)**, *sub nom* **Watson v McEwan (1905)**: an action would lie in *solatium* for wounded feelings arising from disclosure of private information. This would not require proof of patrimonial loss.

**X v Y (1988)**: On the grounds that AIDS patients should feel uninhibited in attending for treatment and that the risk of transmission was negligible, an injunction preventing publication of the names of two doctors with AIDS was granted.

**Stevens v Yorkhill NHS Trust and South Glasgow University Hospital NHS Trust (2006)**: there is support in the case for the use of the *actio iniuriarum* to justify damages for *solatium* for wounded feelings flowing from a breach of confidence.

**Lord Advocate v Scotsman Publications Ltd (1989)**: a duty of confidence applies to third parties where the information was known by the third party to be confidential in nature and was received from a source other than the confider.

**Quilty v Windsor (1999)**: the action against a third party for breach of confidence must contain evidence that the information was transmitted in confidence or was obtained by the defender in the knowledge that it had been communicated in breach of an obligation of confidence.

**R v Department of Health, ex parte Source Informatics Ltd (2000)**: anonymised data is no longer considered confidential. As long as the patient's autonomy was not compromised and their privacy not put at risk, they had no property in the information or right to control its use.

**Durant v Financial Services Authority (2003)**: to fit within the definition of "personal data", the data must impact on the data subject's privacy or have the subject as the focus of the data. The "filing system" in question must be of a high standard.

# 7 THE HUMAN BODY AND TRANSPLANTATION

This chapter is concerned with the ownership and control of the human body and human tissue, including issues of property law, organ donation and transplantation, post mortems and xenotransplantation. It is concerned with both the living human body and the body after death but before cremation or burial, in respect of both the entire human body and parts of the human body. This chapter will also deal with the much-publicised issue of organ retention and unauthorised post-mortem examinations. The various causes of action and remedies will be considered where applicable.

## TRANSPLANTATION

Transplantation of human organs is regulated by recent statutory regime. As this is an area devolved to the Scottish Parliament, there are slight differences between Part 1 of the Human Tissue (Scotland) Act 2006 (the "2006 Act") and the Human Tissue Act 2004 that applies to England and Wales. Where possible, these differences will be pointed out. Both statutes repealed the terms of the Human Tissue Act 1961 for their jurisdiction.

The terms of the 2006 Act continue to support the opt-in system used in UK law, that is to say that parties donating organs must actively and voluntarily opt in to the organ donation system. The opt-out system, in contrast, assumes consent unless a person has actively opted out. The specific terms of the 2006 Act will be discussed below.

Under s 1 of the 2006 Act, Scottish Ministers are under a duty to support and develop transplantation programmes and to ensure that measures are in place regarding supply, storage and use of donated body parts. What is new in the 2006 regime (s 2) is that there are powers for Ministers to provide financial and other support to those providing transplant services or services related to transplantation. Further provisions allow for co-operation with authorities in England and Wales in the provision of services.

The 2006 Act makes provision for transplantation, research, authorisation (of the deceased) and offences in connection with human organ transplantation. These provisions in the 2006 Act on the *use* of body parts for those purposes, do not, however, apply in the following circumstances, which will be discussed further, below:

(1) activities conducted under procurator fiscal authority;

(2) removal of body parts during a post mortem;

(3) retention of tissue samples or organs in certain circumstances set out in the 2006 Act; and

(4) removal, retention or use of body parts of persons who died more than 100 years before the coming into force of s 3 of the 2006 Act.

## Dead bodies

The use of part of a dead body for transplantation or research is governed by the terms of Part 1 of the 2006 Act. Under s 3, tissue or organs ("body parts") may be removed from the deceased and used for transplantation, research, education, training and audit, as long as certain conditions are met and the removal and use is authorised. Authorisation will be discussed below.

The surgeon removing the body part must be satisfied, on physical examination, that the patient is dead. The 2006 Act does not specify how this is to be established, but does stipulate that it may be established only by a registered medical practitioner or someone authorised by regulations to do so. (The definition of death is discussed further in Chapter 8.) It is also necessary to obtain consent from the procurator fiscal for the donation to proceed, in order to ensure that the body is no longer required for his purposes. The appropriate authorisation must have been given for the donation. There is no longer any role under the terms of the 2006 Act for the person in lawful possession of the body.

### Authorisation by the deceased or by their "nearest relative"

It is an offence to remove a body part for use for transplantation, research, etc without authorisation, but defensible if the accused shows a reasonable belief that authorisation had been given. The offence carries a penalty of up to 12 months' imprisonment or a fine of up to level 5 of the standard scale (£5,000) or both, on summary conviction. Conviction on indictment is subject to up to 3 years' imprisonment or a level 5 fine or both.

In recognition of the fact that many people express wishes to friends and family during their lifetime – be it verbally or in writing – the 2006 Act set up a system of authorisation. If a person wants to authorise organ donation after their death, they may register their name on the NHS Organ Donation Register, although even this step will not guarantee that their intentions are clear. Authorisation may be given by an adult prior to their death and may be given verbally. If desired, it may be in writing. If there is an authorisation in force immediately before the adult's death, it will take precedence over a post-mortem examination authorised by that adult or by another person.

Problems emerge where a person has not communicated his wishes as regards organ donation after his death. The 2006 Act provides for a system of authorisation by the deceased's "nearest relative" as defined in the Act. This is allowed under s 7 under certain circumstances such as there being no prior authorisation already in place.

The definition of "nearest relative" is an established hierarchy, which means that recourse should be had initially to the person at the top of the hierarchy and if they are unavailable, to the persons progressively lower down the hierarchy. The hierarchy with respect to the deceased adult is as follows:

1. spouse or civil partner;
2. cohabitee;
3. child;
4. parent;
5. brother or sister;
6. grandparent;
7. grandchild;
8. uncle or aunt;
9. cousin;
10. niece or nephew;
11. friend of long standing (undefined in the 2006 Act).

Half-blood relationships can be treated as whole-blood relationships and step-relationships as natural relationships, although, where there is more than one person in a given category, preference will be given to whole-blood and natural relationships over half-blood and step-relationships respectively.

This hierarchy is slightly different to the system in operation in England and Wales, which gives equal weight to pairs of people (eg step-father and step-mother).

The authorisation given by the deceased's nearest relative must be in writing and signed. Authorisation cannot be given where the nearest relative is aware that the deceased was unwilling for his organs to be donated for transplantation. It is not competent to draw an inference of unwillingness from an absence of a positive declaration.

For authorisation by a nearest relative to be valid, the medical practitioner must be satisfied that the views expressed verbally do in fact apply to the deceased and that they authorise the removal of his organs for transplantation. The practitioner must keep a record of the proceedings.

### Children

The same principles apply to the consent to organ donation of children between the ages of 12 and 16 as apply to consent and confidentiality. They may authorise organ removal after their death for transplantation, research or audit, but this must be done in writing and may be withdrawn only in writing. As with adults, that authorisation is preferred over authorisation for a post mortem. Unless aware of the child's unwillingness for their organs to be so used – and in the absence of written authorisation by the child – the person with parental responsibilities may give authorisation. Authorisation by the person with parental responsibilities or the child's nearest relative must be in writing and signed. It must be in respect of that child and made when the child is older than 12. It must also be witnessed by one person and contain a statement in respect of the child's wishes expressed while still alive.

Authorisation on behalf of children under 12 years of age may be given by the person with parental responsibilities for that child immediately before that child's death. It must be in writing and signed. It is unclear in the legislation what should be done in the event of a disagreement between two parents.

Section 13 of the 2006 Act provides for the preservation of organs after removal and for maintaining the body in a condition that will allow transplantation. Preservation of this sort must take place in a National Health Service facility and permits only the least invasive techniques. This provision does not apply to research, audit and training, although tissue samples may be removed for the purpose of determining the organ's viability (tissue typing).

### Donation under the Anatomy Act 1984

The 2006 Act amended the 1984 Act as applied to Scotland. The subject-matter of the 1984 Act falls within the legislative competence of the Scottish Parliament, as does that of the Human Tissue Act 1961, the Corneal Tissue Act 1986 and the Human Organ Transplants Act 1989.

The 1984 Act governs the use of the cadaver for (macroscopic) anatomical examination for teaching and study purposes. It applies only to those who died after 1988, when the Act came into force. The activities governed under the 1984 Act include acts on the "anatomical specimen", that is the whole body and on parts of the body, such as dissection, removal of parts, prosthesis, etc.

Under s 4 of the 1984 Act, bodies originating outside of Scotland are subject to further provision aimed at ensuring that the law of the country of origin has been complied with. There should have been no previous examination undertaken on imported bodies other than removal of body parts for research, education and training and that examination must be completed within 3 years of the donor's death. Lawful possession is possible thereafter, but only for the purpose of disposal.

Premises carrying out such anatomical examinations are required to be licensed under the 1984 Act. Neither may the activities take place without a death certificate and licence to carry out the examination. Licences are issued by the Scottish Ministers.

Examinations are lawful if a person has given their consent prior to their death. That consent is valid only if the deceased was aged over 12 years when giving it and the consent was given in writing, signed and witnessed by one person.

Following the much-publicised *Bodyworks* exhibition in 2004, the public display of anatomical specimens is prohibited under s 6A of the 1984 Act as added by s 53(9) of the 2006 Act. This prohibition does not include the display of visual images or display for the purpose of paying last respects to the deceased. Under s 11 of the 1984 Act, if an offence is committed, the offender cannot be guilty of any common law offence relating to unlawful anatomical examination.

## The living donor

Not all organ donations are received from deceased donors, but different restrictions have been placed on donations made by living donors under the 2006 Act. The situation in which donors are related to recipients is the same as that in which donor and recipient are unrelated. The same scrutiny applies to all donations.

Unlike its predecessor (the Human Organ Transplants Act 1989), the 2006 Act makes provision for donation of parts of organs such as the liver, regenerative tissue such as bone marrow and for whole organs such as kidneys. While regenerative tissue may be removed form a child, it is an offence under s 17 to remove non-regenerative tissue from a child. It is also an offence under s 17 to remove any organ or tissue from an adult with incapacity, and to use the organs illegally removed. Scottish

Ministers may define exceptions to the offence, but have not yet done so. These offences carry a penalty following summary conviction of up to 12 months' imprisonment or a fine of up to level 5 on the standard scale (£5,000) or both.

## Trafficking

Under s 20 of the 2006 Act it is an offence to traffic in human organs, subject to any exemptions Scottish Ministers may enact. This offence comprises giving or receiving reward for the supply or offer to supply any part of the human body for transplantation. This includes seeking another person to commit the offence, negotiation or offer of supply for reward that contemplates trafficking. Advertising these services is also an offence. These offences also carry a penalty following summary conviction of up to 12 months' imprisonment or a fine of up to level 5 on the standard scale (£5,000) or both.

## Xenotransplantation

Cross-species organ grafting is known as xenotransplantation. The technique involves growing body parts using an animal as the host. The best-known example is the growing of a human ear on the back of a mouse. This subject-matter is reserved to Westminster under Head J2 of Sch 5 to the Scotland Act 1998. Any developments are regulated by an advisory body to the Department of Health called the Xenotransplantation Interim Regulatory Authority. The same rules that apply to consent, negligence and confidentiality will apply to xeno-transplantation procedures.

## POST MORTEMS

Post-mortem examinations take place under the authority of the procurator fiscal in certain circumstances. They are also conducted by hospitals to determine morbidity and cause of death. The practice of taking and retaining tissue samples and organs of children following post-mortem examination, and doing so without informing the parents or gaining their consent, led to calls for tighter regulation. This led to some of the provisions in the 2006 Act, following recommendations of the Independent Review Group on Retention of Organs at Post Mortem and related matters. It also led to a consideration by the courts of the cause of action available to those parents and to appropriate heads of damages.

## Civil liability in Scots law for affront under the *actio iniuriarum*

Three Scottish post-mortem cases from the early 20th century suggested the possibility of an action in damages for *solatium* brought by relatives of those on whom an unauthorised post-mortem examination or organ removal and retention was carried out. These cases were *Pollock* v *Workman* (1900), *Conway* v *Dalziel* (1901) and *Hughes* v *Robertson* (1912). The action is based on affront. This is a distinct form of action to that for psychiatric injury, which is based on "nervous shock" at learning of the wrong perpetrated. It constitutes a form of personal injury.

The interpretation of the three post-mortem cases determined the outcome of the organ retention cases of the 21st century. All three cases involved post-mortem examinations instructed by a solicitor with a view to establishing cause of death, but *Conway* v *Dalziel* also involved the retention of organs. In that case, two medical practitioners retained the organs of a deceased workman. His widow sued his former employer for wounded feelings. The case failed on a technicality, but there was indication in the judgment that without the technical error, the case for *solatium* may have had more merit. There is also some authority in these cases for the proposition that a claim lies in *solatium* rather than in nervous shock following negligence. This is supported by the judgment in *AB* v *Leeds Teaching Hospital NHS Trust* (2005), discussed below, in which the court did not consider the Scottish post-mortem cases to have been founded on negligence. The difference between the two actions is that the former requires an affront, while the latter requires a personal injury.

The action for *solatium* for affront under the *actio iniuriarum* is brought by the surviving relatives and is based on the unauthorised interference with the body of the deceased, causing an affront to the *dignitas* of the pursuer.

*Stevens* v *Yorkhill NHS Trust Hospital and South Glasgow University Hospital NHS Trust* (2006) involved a claim for *solatium* following the alleged affront to the feelings of parents of a child whose organs were removed and retained at post mortem. The court found that Scots law recognises the claim for *solatium* as based on the *actio iniuriarum*. It was also found that the defender owed the pursuer a duty of care, despite the pursuer not having made averments in support of the existence of a doctor–patient relationship. The duty was owed at the time when consent was sought to the carrying out of a post mortem. It was based on proximity between the doctor and the pursuer. The duty of care included disclosure that removal and retention of organs may take place. The duty was breached, leading to liability in damages.

## Civil liability in English law in negligence for psychiatric harm

The English case of *AB* v *Leeds Teaching Hospital NHS Trust* (2005) was the lead case among several which involved the unauthorised retention of organs of deceased children at post-mortem examination. The case was litigated according to established principles and tests applied to nervous shock cases. It was based on the allegation that psychiatric harm was a foreseeable consequence of a failure to counsel the plaintiffs that the post-mortem examination may involve removal and retention of organs. As a nervous shock case, a close tie of love and affection between the claimant and the primary victim is required, as well as a short space of time between the event and the psychiatric injury.

In *AB* v *Leeds*, the court found that the parents of the deceased child were primary victims, unlike the secondary victims envisaged in nervous shock cases such as *Alcock* v *Chief Constable of South Yorkshire Police* (1992). The child could not have been a victim, as no duty of care is owed after death. It was therefore important to determine whether a duty of care was owed to the parents. The court found that there was a doctor–patient relationship between the parents and the hospital and that the provision of information was not merely an administrative matter. It was considered fair, just and reasonable to find that there was a duty of care in the circumstances.

On the provision of information, the court found both the *Bolam* and *Bolitho* judgments (discussed in Chapters 4 and 5 of this book) to be relevant in determining whether the hospital's omission was reasonable. It found that the duty of care included provision of information on what the post-mortem examination would involve and that it was a breach of duty to fail to inform the parents that organs may be retained. Even so, not all of the claims were successful; success depended on the degree of foreseeability of harm and on proof of causation.

On the basis of this case and considering the nervous shock case law, the following requirements are essential:

- the resulting psychiatric illness must be a foreseeable result of the specific act or omission relied upon by the claimant;
- there must be a sufficient likelihood that the psychiatric illness will occur;

- it must be foreseeable that psychiatric illness would have been suffered by that particular claimant;
- the standard of care is judged by the standard of the consultant paediatrician rather than the consultant psychiatrist, as the defender is in the former occupation.

## Post mortems under the Human Tissue (Scotland) Act 2006

Part 2 of the 2006 Act provides a framework for the authorisation of hospital post mortems. These are distinguished from anatomical examinations performed under the 1984 Act. Neither does the 2006 Act apply to the bodies of those who have been dead for 100 years or more.

Section 23 defines a post-mortem examination as the "examination of the body of a deceased person involving its dissection and the removal of organs, tissue sample, blood (or any material derived from blood) or other body fluid".

### Authorisation

Similar principles that apply elsewhere in the 2006 Act apply to authorisation for post-mortem examinations. As such, adults may before death give authorisation for removal and retention of organs for transplantation, research and audit after their death. Separate and similar provisions apply to mature minors and children as apply to organ donation, etc. These have been set out above.

The authorisation may be either written or verbal, although verbal authorisation requires to be given in the presence of two witnesses and written authorisations must be withdrawn in writing. Verbal authorisations may be withdrawn verbally, in the presence of two witnesses.

Adults may nominate a person or persons to give authorisation on their behalf. Nominees must be appointed in writing, with the appointment signed and witnessed by one person who is not the nominee. The witness must certify that the adult (or the child if that is the case) in their opinion understands the effect of the nomination.

The same hierarchy of "nearest relative" is applicable to this part of the 2006 Act. In the absence of an authorisation by the adult or the appointment of a nominee, the deceased's "nearest relative" may give authorisation. This must be in writing and can be withdrawn, but only in writing in the presence of a witness.

The mature minor may also give such authorisation. It must be in writing, signed and witnessed by two people. The same nomination provisions apply to mature minors as apply to adults. What is different is the use of the "nearest relative" hierarchy, which in the case of the mature minor means that authority rests with the minor's parents. Such authorisation made on behalf of the minor must be in writing, be in respect of that particular minor, authorise the activity in question and be signed on behalf of the child. It must also be witnessed by one witness. A statement is required to be added to the effect that in the opinion of the person with parental rights and responsibilities, the child understood the nature and effect of the authorisation.

Authorisation may be given in respect of minors under the age of 12 for removal and retention of organs. This may be given by the person with parental rights and responsibilities immediately before the child's death. It must be written, signed and witnessed by two people. The same applies to its withdrawal.

Under the 2006 Act, organs removed and retained are different to tissue samples removed and retained. Any part of the body removed and retained following proper authorisation will form part of the deceased's medical records. They may be removed and retained for the purposes of audit, education, training and research following proper authorisation. It is an offence to perform a post-mortem examination without authorisation, although it will be a defence to show reasonable belief that authorisation had been given. Conviction on summary procedure carries a penalty of up to 12 months' imprisonment or a fine of up to level 5 on the standard scale (£5,000) or both. On indictment, the penalty is a fine of up to level 5 or up to 3 years' imprisonment or both.

### Interface with procurator fiscal purposes

As the 2006 Act relates to hospital post mortems only, it does not apply to post-mortem examinations conducted for the procurator fiscal's purposes. The procurator fiscal is required to examine the body of a person suspected to have been involved in criminal activity and must inquire into all sudden, suspicious or unexplained deaths.

That said, s 26 of the 2006 Act requires that if there is reason to believe that the body of the deceased is required for procurator fiscal purposes, a hospital post mortem may proceed only following permission from the fiscal. This may be verbal, but must later be confirmed in writing. Organ and tissue samples no longer required by the procurator fiscal become part of the deceased's medical records. Samples removed and retained for procurator fiscal purposes may be subsequently used for the purposes of education, training and research. This does not require authorisation.

## PROPERTY RIGHTS

The ownership and control of the whole or parts of the human body are regulated by the common law. As such Scots property law as it applies to corporeal movables is applicable.

### The whole body

Property law is concerned with things rather than natural persons. This means that people can be the subject rather than the object of real rights. While one may donate parts or the whole of the body after death or parts of the body while alive, one is prohibited from selling one's body or body parts.

The question arises whether it is possible in law to own a corpse before its burial. There is some civil law authority in *McGruer, Petr* (1898), *per* Sheriff-Substitute Scott-Moncrieff, to the effect that the answer to that question is no. The dead body, therefore, is *ex commercium*. It is for this reason that it not possible to steal a corpse once buried, as theft can be committed only on owned objects (the crime in question is the violation of sepulchres).

While there is no obligation to dispose of a dead body in Scots law (unlike English law), there is an entitlement of next-of-kin, relatives or executors to arrange for the burial. If they do not make arrangements, the local authority has a duty to do so under the National Assistance Act 1948.

While there are no rights of ownership, there is a right of possession. According to *Evans* v *McIntyre* (1980), and *Rees* v *Hughes* (1946), this right is held by the deceased's executor, as it is that person who would decide on arrangements for the burial. Yet, problems arise where no executor has been appointed. In that case, the nearest relative may enjoy that right. Although there is no authority on the point, it is the nearest relative who would have an action in *solatium* for unauthorised interference with the corpse, so arguably they who would have rights of possession in the corpse.

### Body parts

#### Parts taken from a living person

Because body parts are capable of transfer through donation, property law is applicable (although certain transactions, such as trade, are prohibited, as discussed below). There is authority to the effect that a part removed from the body is capable of ownership by the person from whose body it was removed and an abandoned thing becomes Crown property if it was capable of ownership. There is also a statutory duty of reasonable care on the possessor of lost or abandoned property, under the Civic Government (Scotland) Act 1982. There is a duty to report the fact of having taken possession of the thing. There is certainly an untested argument that the property law rules of occupation should confer original title on the first occupier of the thing.

The American case of *Moore* v *Regents of the University of California* (1990) dealt with the ownership of a cell line developed from a sample of cells taken from a patient. A patent was sought. This application was opposed by Moore. The court was reluctant to find that there was property in living human cells, but did find for the patient on the basis of breach of a fiduciary duty and lack of informed consent.

In the Scots law of *specificatio*, a person who in good faith makes a new thing out of other things, through skill, acquires ownership of the new thing. That person has a duty to compensate the source or the person who had ownership before the *specificatio*, to the tune of the value of that part prior to incorporation. There is, however, no authority on this point in respect of human organs and body parts for a remedy, sought by the original possessor. Neither is the doctor–patient relationship a fiduciary one, as it was in *Moore*.

It is worth noting in closing that under Art 21 of the European Convention on Human Rights and Biomedicine, "the human body and its parts shall not, as such, give rise to financial gain".

### Parts taken from a dead person

The organ retention cases are in point here. In these cases, tissue samples and organs of deceased children were retained by hospitals without authorisation. In England, *AB* v *Leeds Teaching Hospital NHS Trust* (2005) was heard under the tort of wrongful interference with the parents' right of possession, which was to depend on whether the parents had a right of possession in the first place.

Under Scots law, the child's surviving relatives have an action in delict under the *action iniuriarum* for *solatium* for affront. This was discussed above, in relation to post mortems.

The difference from English law is that in Scots law the relationship with the deceased is important, while in English law the body parts acquire characteristics of property through skilful dissection and the production of tissue slides.

Intellectual property in body parts requires that the product be novel for a patent to be awarded, yet under the European Patent Convention this would not be possible in the case of biological material. However, the Patent Convention applies to "life", which does not cover human cell lines and DNA. For these, the applicable European Directive is that on biotechnological inventions. Article 6 requires substantial benefit to humans or animals. It also prohibits patents that involve human cloning, modifying human genetic identity and industrial or commercial use of human embryos.

## Essential Facts

*Transplantation*

- Regulation of transplantation is devolved to the Scottish Parliament and regulated under the Human Tissue (Scotland) Act 2006.
- Organs may be removed from the deceased and used for transplantation, research, education, training and audit, as long as the patient is dead and the removal and use are authorised.
- It is an offence to act without authorisation.
- Authorisation may be given by the deceased before his death or by the deceased's nearest relative.
- A hierarchy of "nearest relatives" is set out in the 2006 Act for the purpose of authorisation.
- The same principles apply to the consent to organ donation of children between the ages of 12 and 16 as apply to consent and confidentiality. Authorisation is competent if the mature minor understands the nature and consequences of what he is authorising.
- The person with parental responsibility for the child (and the mature minor, in the absence of the mature minor's authorisation) may give authorisation on behalf of the child.
- Various rules are in place as to whether consent and withdrawal require to be in writing, signed and witnessed.
- The Anatomy Act 1984, as amended by the 2006 Act, governs the use of the cadaver for macroscopic anatomical examination for teaching and study purposes.
- The 1984 Act makes provision for the premises licensed to carry out research and teaching using cadavers, including those not originating in Scotland.
- Under the 1984 Act, consent to the use of a person's body after their death is valid only if made after the deceased was 12 years of age and

had knowledge and understanding of the implications of his consent. Consent must be in writing, signed and witnessed.

- Different restrictions are placed on donations by living donors, under the 2006 Act.
- Under the 2006 Act, live donations are provided for in respect of regenerating tissue and parts of organs, although it is an offence to remove regenerative tissue from a child under 17 years of age or to remove organs from an adult with incapacity.
- It is an offence to give, receive, offer, advertise or act as an agent for, reward in respect of human organs. This is defined as trafficking in human organs.

*Post-mortem examinations*

- Post-mortem examinations take place under the authority of the procurator fiscal where the person is suspected to have been involved in criminal activity; the fiscal must inquire into all sudden, suspicious or unexplained deaths.
- They also take place within hospital to ascertain cause of death, etc. These are regulated under the 2006 Act.
- The same principles of authorisation apply to hospital post-mortem examinations as apply to organ donation for transplantation, research, audit and teaching. As such, authorisation may be given by the deceased before his death, by his nominee or, in the absence of authorisation by either, by the deceased's "nearest relative" in the hierarchy set out in the 2006 Act.
- Different provisions apply to whether authorisation and withdrawal of authorisation may be verbal or is required to be in writing, signed and witnessed.
- Authorisation may be given by the mature minor, in the absence of which it may be given by the person with parental rights and responsibilities, as is the case with children.
- Body parts and tissue samples properly removed and retained form part of the deceased's medical records.
- It is an offence to perform a post-mortem examination without proper authorisation.
- In English law, removal and retention of tissue and samples of the deceased gives rise to an action in negligence based on nervous shock suffered by the parents as primary victims.

- In Scots law, the unauthorised removal and retention of tissue and organs gives rise to an action in damages for *solatium* for affront under the *actio iniuriarum*.
- As a result of the circumstances that gave rise to the case law, Part 2 of the 2006 Act provides a framework for the authorisation of hospital post mortems.
- Authorisation for post-mortem examination follows similar rules to those set out in respect of organ donation. These rules apply to authorisation, nominees, "nearest relative" and the rules applicable to minors and mature minors.
- Further rules apply to whether the authorisation and its withdrawal must be in writing, signed and witnessed.

*Property rights*

- The ownership and control of the whole or parts of the human body are regulated by the common law.
- The whole dead body is outside of commerce and hence not capable of ownership or theft.
- The deceased's next-of-kin, relatives or executors are entitled to arrange for the burial.
- While there are no rights of ownership, there is a right of possession of the whole human body, and hence that person would have an action in *solatium* for unauthorised interference with the corpse.
- Because body parts are capable of transfer through donation, property law is applicable to them.
- There is an untested argument that the property law rules of occupation should confer original title on the first occupier of a thing.
- In the Scots law of *specificatio*, a person who in good faith makes a new thing out of other things, through skill, acquires ownership of the new thing, but there is no authority on this point in respect of human organs and body parts, for a remedy sought by the original possessor.
- Article 21 of the European Convention on Human Rights and Biomedicine reads: "the human body and its parts shall not, as such, give rise to financial gain."
- The organ retention cases are applicable to body parts taken from the deceased.

## Essential Cases

**McGruer, Petr (1898)**: It is not possible in law to own a corpse before its burial.

**Evans v McIntyre (1980)**, citing **Rees v Hughes (1946)**: possession rights are held by the deceased's executor as it is that person who would decide on arrangements for the burial.

**Moore v Regents of the University of California (1990)**: the court was reluctant to find that there was property in living human cells.

**AB v Leeds Teaching Hospital NHS Trust (2005)**: tissue samples and organs of deceased children were retained by hospitals without authorisation. The case was heard under the tort of wrongful interference with the parents' right of possession. It was the lead case among several which alleged that psychiatric injury had been suffered as a result of the negligent failure to inform of the possibility that tissue and organs may be retained at post mortem. The court found that there was a doctor–patient relationship between the parents and the hospital. Both the *Bolam* and *Bolitho* judgments were relevant in determining whether the hospital's omission was reasonable. The duty of care included provision of information on what the post-mortem examination would involve and failure to inform the parents that organs may be retained was a breach of that duty.

**Stevens v Yorkhill NHS Trust Hospital and South Glasgow University Hospital NHS Trust (2006)**: in the Scottish organ retention case it was found that the true juridical basis of the claim was in an action in damages for *solatium* based on the *actio iniuriarum*. The duty of care was based on proximity between pursuer and doctor. That duty included disclosure that removal and retention of organs might take place. The duty was breached, leading to liability in damages.

# 8 MEDICAL FUTILITY, EUTHANASIA AND ASSISTED SUICIDE

Several medico–legal issues are raised at the end of life. Many relate to the improved ability of technology to prolong life, but others relate to the expectation that technology might be used to hasten death. These questions lead to others surrounding medical futility and the prospect of treatment continuing to provide a benefit. Other questions are raised surrounding assisted suicide; the value and authority of advance statements; and euthanasia, all of which beg further questions as to the values attributed to human life.

## DEATH IN LAW

It was clear from parts of Chapter 7 that death is essential for certain activities, such as some organ donations, to take place legally. Yet, death is not defined in statute in Scotland. Because natural death is a process rather than an event in the medical sense, it is at times important in law to establish a point after which a person is said to have died. Several possibilities exist, based on the functioning of the heart, lungs and brain. While the first two can be maintained artificially, the third can not.

Yet, even if the brain stem is irreparably damaged and the patient is in a permanent vegetative state (PVS), medico–legal questions may be raised as to whether the patient can be "allowed to die". It is for this reason that the PVS cases are instructive when considering the definition of death.

In *Law Hospital NHS Trust* v *Lord Advocate* (1996), Janet Johnson had been in a PVS for 3 years without prospect of recovery or awareness of her surroundings. She remained medically alive by artificial means. In *Finlayson* v *HM Advocate* (1979), the patient was in a PVS following an injection of controlled drugs. The accused had been charged with culpable homicide. Both cases involved the maintenance of life by artificial means, raising the question of the ending of that life. In *Finlayson* it was considered that switching off the life-support machinery did not break the chain of causation between the actions of the accused and the death of the victim, yet it was also assumed that the victim was legally dead as far as the criminal law was concerned only once life-support was discontinued. From this it is reasonable to assume that death occurs when the whole brain or the brain stem is dead.

## FUTILITY AND INCAPACITY

"Futility" refers to demands by or on behalf of the patient for treatments that will not serve the desired medical ends or not be in the patient's best medical interests. It is not exclusive to end-of-life decisions, as it may also be invoked, for example, in connection with non-treatment of newborn infants. What is important is that "futility" refers to the medical prognosis rather than any question of resources. It follows that the patient's wishes, autonomy, interests and quality of life are central to decisions on futility.

### Selective non-treatment of children

Children are not legally capable of making treatment decisions. It follows that a "substituted judgement" test cannot apply because the patient was never capable of making a decision on his own behalf and hence the question, what they would have decided cannot be asked. The same applies to legally incapable adults, as discussed below. Different legal regimes operate in England and in Scotland, with the English law governed largely by the common law and Scots law set out in the Children (Scotland) Act 1995.

### English common law and human rights

In the absence of Scottish authority, English decisions on children born with severe disabilities will be persuasive. The case law indicates that a "best interests" test has been used in balancing the quality of a disabled or shortened life against ending that life. Consent to surgery was refused by the parents of a child born with Down's Syndrome and an intestinal complaint in *Re B (a minor) (wardship: medical treatment)* (1992). The surgery may have given the child a life expectancy of 20–30 years. The court found that the operation should be performed, as the expected quality of life outweighed life's destruction.

These cases often deal with the distinction between actively hastening death and passively allowing the patient to die. A case dealing with this active/passive distinction was *Re C (a minor) (wardship: medical treatment)* (1989). In that case the child was brain damaged and terminally ill. The decision in *Re B* was distinguished in finding that the child's welfare was paramount. An operation to treat the child in order to allow a peaceful death was permitted.

Similarly, in the leading decision of *Re J (a minor) (wardship: medical treatment)* (1992), the child was not dying, but was disabled. Placed on a ventilator following premature birth, the child was expected to live no longer than his teens and to do so in a state of limited intellectual ability. The court had to decide the permissible course of action should J collapse again. The question before the court was whether to approve the withholding of life-prolonging treatment. The court would not allow active steps to be taken to hasten death. It used a "substituted judgement" test to ask what J might have decided and found that it was not in his best interests to ventilate him if he was to stop breathing, unless it was considered medically appropriate to do so.

This first *Re J* was approved in another case of that name: *Re J (a minor) (wardship: medical treatment)* (1992). The latter case used the "best interests" test to assess future quality of life and sanctioned medical decision-making in such cases. That courts will not tell members of the medical profession how to perform their role was emphasised in *Re C (a baby)* (1996). The case involved a baby who became brain damaged from meningitis. The court approved of the medical expert agreement that it was not in her best interests to be ventilated artificially. As such, courts will not *require* doctors to treat children in such circumstances.

These decisions pre-dated the enactment of the Human Rights Act 1998, by which point the "best interests" test had become accepted as appropriate in these circumstances. Certain Articles of the European Convention on Human Rights, as enacted by the 1998 Act, became important too. These are Art 2 on the right to life, Art 3 prohibiting inhuman and degrading treatment and Art 8 on respect for private life. In *A National Health Service Trust* v *D* (2000), a hospital sought declaration that non-resuscitation of a 19-month-old child with irreversible lung disease would be consistent with Arts 2 and 3. The court found that Art 2 would not be infringed if non-treatment was in the child's best interests. In addition, the non-treatment decision by its nature protected the child from inhuman and degrading treatment, being in her best medical interests. It was found in *Glass* v *United Kingdom* (2004) that treatment contrary to parental wishes and without court authority violated Art 8.

The case of *Re A (children) (conjoined twins: surgical separation)* (2000) dealt with both selective non-treatment and treatment in the child's best interests. It involved the separation of conjoined twins that would allow one to live at the expense of the death of the other. The separation was opposed by the parents, who relied on Art 2 of the ECHR that disallows intentional deprivation of life. Because surgery on Mary would end her life, the court could not authorise it. The two children were considered separate persons even although Mary's life depended on her sister Jodie. It was found that the benefits to Jodie outweighed Mary's inevitable death.

It was, however, considered impossible to invoke the best interests test in respect of both girls; the court considered its decision in terms of the lesser of two evils. It was found that "best interests" should include emotional and welfare interests.

### The Children (Scotland) Act 1995

Although no analogous decisions have been reported in Scotland, there have been a number of fatal accident inquiries of interest. These have indicated that where a decision to not resuscitate a child was made in the child's best interests and constituted a reasonable clinical decision, the determination of the inquiry has supported the non-treatment decision. Similar decisions have been reached in respect of the decision against giving a liver transplant to a teenage girl.

Where there is a conflict of views between the parents and the medical practitioners involved with the child's care, the decision should be referred to the courts. This should be done through a specific issue order under the Children (Scotland) Act 1995. Both the person with parental rights and responsibilities and the medical practitioner may apply in their capacity as persons having an interest under s 11. Orders made under the 1995 Act will take precedence over common law orders of the court. A "best interests" test would be brought to bear on a decision to withdraw life-prolonging treatment from a child younger than 16.

## Withdrawing or withholding treatment from adults

As mentioned above, it is appropriate to use a "substituted judgement" test in making a non-treatment decision on behalf of the adult *incapax*, whereas this is not appropriate in the case of children. This is because adults will have been legally capable prior to entering the permanent vegetative state, for example, which will render such an assessment possible, whereas children will not have been capable in the legal sense.

### The permanent vegetative state

A person is in a permanent vegetative state (PVS) if they do not have and are never going to recover awareness of their surroundings or who show no response to tactile, visual, auditory or noxious stimuli, or have no awareness of language or ability to communicate. As accurate diagnosis is crucial, *Practice Note (persistent vegetative state: withdrawal of treatment)* (1996) requires evidence from two independent medical practitioners that the patient is, in fact, in a permanent vegetative state. In PVS situations the "substituted judgement" test is important, as is the doctrine of "double effect" which considers it acceptable to administer a palliative treatment even although its effect will be to hasten death (eg morphine in high doses).

The English case of *Airedale NHS Trust v Bland* (1993) followed the Hillsborough football stadium disaster in which many died or were injured. Anthony Bland suffered brain damage caused by lack of oxygen and had no hope of recovery. Although he could breathe on his own, he was insensate and was fed through a gastric tube. He did not feel pain. The health authority was supported by his parents in its application to discontinue feeding and hydration. The court considered this to amount to medical treatment and therefore to fall within the category of decisions surrounding withdrawal of life-sustaining treatment.

The distinction between acts and omissions was important to the decision of the court. It held that treatment could lawfully be withdrawn in the patient's best medical interests where it was futile to prolong life. The House of Lords, however, found that Bland did not have any interests in a PVS. Neither would withdrawal of treatment be a criminal act where there was no positive duty to maintain life. For this reason, there would be no violation of Art 2 ECHR. Withdrawal of treatment, on the other hand, would mean that he would be allowed to die of his existing injuries.

In Scotland, the Court of Session may authorise a medical practitioner to withdraw life-prolonging treatment from a patient in a PVS if continuing with that treatment is not in the patient's interests. In *Law Hospital NHS Trust v Lord Advocate* (1996), Janet Johnstone was in a PVS following a failed suicide attempt 4 years prior to the case. The question before the court was whether to authorise the withdrawal of life-sustaining treatment. The court had the benefit of the decision in the *Bland* case. As in *Bland*, Janet Johnstone was fed artificially, was unaware of her surroundings and had no prospect of recovery. Continuing with hydration and feeding would be of no benefit to her and hence was futile.

As was the case in the *Bland* judgment, it was found that Janet had no best interests that could be served by any treatment decision and that the declaration sought was lawful and treatment could be withdrawn. The court set out a clear statement of the appropriate procedure to be followed in such cases in obtaining authority from the Court of Session, under its *parens patriae* jurisdiction, for withdrawal of futile life-sustaining treatment. Aside from rules of procedure, the judgment specified that the following should be lodged with the petition:

- at least two medical reports on the patient's condition, describing the proposed course of action and the steps that will be taken to allow death to occur with dignity;

- a statement of the first diagnosis of PVS (British Medical Association Guidelines advise that treatment should continue for at least the first 12 months of the patient's insentience);
- a statement of any views on treatment decisions that the patient may have expressed prior to going into a PVS.

The court should be asked to appoint a *curator ad litem* to act on behalf of the patient (as the petition will be brought by the hospital or family of the patient).

This statement of practice is set out at the end of reports of the First Division's decision in *Law Hospital NHS Trust* v *Lord Advocate* (1996). The judgment also set out the following common law principles to be followed in making negative treatment decisions on behalf of patients in a PVS:

1. It is not competent for the Court of Session to issue a declarator in respect of the criminal or otherwise nature of the withdrawal of treatment. A declarator should be confined to the civil law consequences. Any decision to prosecute on the same set of facts remains with the Lord Advocate. Following the *Law Hospital* decision, the Lord Advocate in a statement said he would not authorise prosecution of a medical practitioner who acts in good faith and with the authority of the Court of Session to cause life-sustaining treatment to be withdrawn from a patient in PVS, leading to the death of that patient.

2. Although a declarator was competent, it was also possible to petition the court to invoke its inherent *parens patriae* jurisdiction. Authorising discontinuing treatment through this route and using the "best interests" test will resolve any questions of delictual liability arising from the acts or omissions of medical practitioners.

3. However, neither procedure is strictly necessary where the discontinuance of treatment is in the patient's best interests. That said, without the court's approval, there is no guarantee that prosecution will not follow.

### A note on best interests

It will have been noted that there appears to be a paradox in operation in applying the "best interests" test while at the same time holding that the patient in a PVS has no best interests. Yet the courts in both *Bland* and *Law Hospital* approved of its use. It is not about best interests as much as it is about whether continuing with life-prolonging treatment will serve any interest at all, where treatment is futile. Neither is it about whether the patient's interests will be served by allowing him to die. Rather, it is about whether it is in his interest to be kept alive.

If treatment will serve no interest, there will be no balance to be struck. Seen this way, the "best interests" test is applied in the negative sense. What is critical is that the wishes of the patient's family and the issue of resources should not obscure a decision that should be taken from the point of view of the patient in a PVS.

What is important is the question to be asked and answered by the court. The courts in *Bland* found that rather than asking whether the action should be taken that will kill the patient, the question should be whether the medical practitioner should continue to provide treatment that will prolong the patient's life. A problem with this approach is that arguably the two questions are inseparable and to try to separate them is an act of semantics.

### Acts and omissions

The distinction between acts and omissions is an important policy device of the courts, though it, too, may be a matter of semantics. In *Bland* the court found that removal of nutrition and hydration was an omission rather than an act. Whereas the *mens rea* was present, the *actus reus* giving rise to a murder conviction was absent in the case of an omission where there is no duty to act. The same distinction is important in understanding the active ending of a patient's life through medication (euthanasia or physician-assisted suicide) and withdrawal of the means supporting life, even although the consequence is the same, as the death of the patient will result. However, it may be that the two are therefore morally indistinguishable.

### The Adults with Incapacity (Scotland) Act 2000

Under the Adults with Incapacity (Scotland) Act 2000 (the "2000 Act") "medical treatment" includes any medical procedure designed to safeguard or promote physical or mental health. There is authority under Part 5 of the 2000 Act for the medical practitioner primarily responsible for the care of a patient to do what is reasonable in the circumstances in relation to medical treatment in order to safeguard the patient's physical and mental health. What is excluded form Part 5 is "negative" treatment.

Section 47 of the 2000 Act, being without prejudice to any common law provision, works to maintain the authority of the decision in *Law Hospital* in respect of patients in a PVS. That said, the 2000 Act allows "proxy decision-makers" to intervene in the affairs of the incapable adult where that intervention will confer some benefit on the patient that can not be achieved by another method and having taken into account any previously expressed wishes of the patient. It may be possible, then, to apply for an intervention order under s 53 of the 2000 Act, directing a specific action and to do so in matters addressed by the court in the *Law Hospital* case. It is considered that a sheriff would be unlikely to grant such an application because of (1) the act/omission dichotomy and (2) the fact that the Scottish Law Commission deliberately excluded from the legislation the withholding or withdrawing of treatment from adult patients in a PVS.

It is perhaps significant that the 2000 Act does not employ the concept of "best interests". This is because the "best interest" test was considered by the Scottish Law Commission to be more appropriate to children, whereas the adults falling within the scope of the 2000 Act will have possessed full capacity prior to the incapacity that caused them to fall within the terms of the legislation. This rationale was accepted by the Scottish Executive in its drafting of the legislation.

## ADVANCE STATEMENTS

It will be remembered that the judgment in *Law Hospital NHS Trust* v *Lord Advocate* (1996) specified that in future one of documents to be lodged with a petition to the court seeking authorisation of withdrawal of treatment should be a statement of any views on treatment decisions that the patient may have expressed prior to going into a PVS. This may be considered a form of advance statement, also known as an advance directive or living will. It amounts to a decision on treatment before the medical need arises.

Such a statement must be made when the patient is competent to do so and acted upon when the patient is no longer competent. An example may be found in *Re C (adult: refusal of medical treatment)* (1994), in which an adult patient with schizophrenia refused an amputation even although he might have died of gangrene as a result. Because his refusal was made during a lucid interval, it was held to be competent when he lacked capacity. Conversely, on the authority of *Re J (a minor) (wardship: medical treatment)* (1990), a patient's request to act contrary to the medical practitioner's clinical judgement or to the patient's best interests will not be legally binding.

Although the Scottish Law Commission recommended legislative reform, the Scottish Executive left the matter out of what became the Adults with Incapacity (Scotland) Act 2000. In England and Wales, on the other hand, advance statements have been given statutory authority by the Mental Capacity Act 2005. The effect is that recourse needs to be had to the common law and the persuasive recognition in the English decision in the *Bland* case that advance refusals of treatment will be competent if made by a legally capable person who was properly informed of the consequences of the decision they were making and not subject to undue influence. It should also be a statement made in respect of the actual treatment being refused.

The Mental Health (Care and Treatment) (Scotland) Act 2003 deals with advanced directives only in respect of compulsory treatment. The Act sets out procedures to be followed in order to express treatment preferences that will be acted upon in the patient's incapacity. The statement must be signed and witnessed and the witness must attest that the patient was capable of making the statement that they made. It may also be withdrawn while the patient is capable of so doing. "Capacity" under the 2003 Act has the same meaning as that defined under s 1(6) of the 2000 Act, ie the capacity to make, communicate, or understand decisions or retain memory of decisions made in respect of the patient's care.

Although the statement will not be legally binding, the Mental Health Tribunal for Scotland is charged with "giving effect" to the advance statement. When considering a treatment order, the Tribunal must "have regard to" any advance statement made. The person treating the adult with incapacity must also have regard to any advance statement made by the patient. Where treatment is given that runs contrary to the terms of an advance statement, a statement of the treatment given must be recorded and added to the patient's medical records. A statement of reasons for acting contrary to the terms of the advance statement must also be added. Under s 276 of the 2003 Act, copies must be sent to the service user (patient), their named person (if any), welfare attorney or guardian and to the Mental Welfare Commission for Scotland.

## ASSISTED SUICIDE

Because suicide and attempted suicide are not criminal offences in Scotland, a person cannot be guilty art and part of either. Yet, killing a person at their request will amount to murder, in terms of *HM Advocate* v *Rutherford* (1947).

Although there is no primary authority on whether it is criminal to help another end his life, criminal liability may follow assisting another to do so. This may be on the grounds of recklessly endangering human life or of culpable homicide. It may amount to murder if the intention of committing an act was to end the life of the victim. This would, however, beg the question of whether the action of the victim in ending his life amounted to a *novus actus interveniens* breaking the chain of causation between the act of the accused and the victim's death.

Assisted suicide may happen through a positive act, by providing the means to commit suicide, giving information or advice to do so or through an omission to prevent the person from ending his life. Assistance may be given by another person such as a family member or indeed by a medical practitioner (physician-assisted suicide).

## Challenge under the European Convention on Human Rights

The English case of *R (on the application of Pretty)* v *Director of Public Prosecutions* (2002) involved a woman with motor neurone disease who sought the court's assurance that her husband could help her to die at the time of her choosing, without facing prosecution under the Suicide Act 1961. Dianne Pretty challenged the decision of the Director of Public Prosecutions that he did not have the power to decline to prosecute an offence in advance of the commission of that offence.

Dianne Pretty's claim failed. It had been based on the European Convention on Human Rights. The court found that Art 2 (on the right to life) was intended to *prevent* another person depriving one of life. Article 3 protects dignity in life, but does not grant a right to die with dignity. While Art 8 protects the right to private and family life, interference with that right must be in accordance with the law and she was prevented in law from her proposed course of action. Article 9 protects a freedom of belief; it was held that this does not extend to a belief in assisted suicide. As such, the European Court of Human Rights found that there was no infringement of the Convention.

There is no Scottish precedent on this issue. Whether the decision would be followed in Scotland would depend on the compatibility of the existing common law with the ECHR. Although it is technically possible to prosecute for the offence of wicked endangerment of life, someone who provides advice on the means to take their life would not fit the scenario envisaged by Dianne Pretty who, because of her medical condition, would need help to fulfil her wishes.

## Physician-assisted suicide

The term "physician-assisted suicide" is applied where, at the patient's request, a medical practitioner helps end the life of a patient who is incapable of doing so himself. The medical practitioner effectively assisting a suicide may have recourse to the defence of double effect, as discussed above, in which a drug was administered as a palliative that also had the effect of hastening death (eg morphine). Although there is no case law directly in point, the *Pretty* judgment may arguably apply to the medical practitioner.

In *Re B (adult: refusal of medical treatment)* (2002), an artificially ventilated tetraplaegic woman sought a declaration that artificially keeping her alive amounted to a trespass. The court found in her favour because the adult patient of full capacity may validly refuse treatment and artificial ventilation constitutes medical treatment. The case is not, strictly speaking, one of physician assisted suicide as it applies the same principles of consent and refusal considered in Chapter 5.

## EUTHANASIA

Euthanasia may be defined as putting someone to death in a compassionate manner following his suffering. It may be used interchangeably with "assisted dying", although this has already been discussed separately. A distinction should be drawn, from the point of view of the person performing the act of compassion, between active euthanasia (killing) and passive euthanasia (allowing death). A further distinction is possible from the patient's point of view: euthanasia may be voluntary, involuntary or non-voluntary, depending on whether the patient can and has expressed an opinion on the issue of his death.

The subject is not specifically regulated in Scotland. It does not fall within the terms of either the Adults with Incapacity (Scotland) Act 2000 or the Mental Health (Care and Treatment) (Scotland) Act 2003. Neither is there specific mention of the question of euthanasia being reserved to Westminster under the Scotland Act 1998. This may seem odd, considering that there is specific mention of human fertilisation and embryology and of abortion being reserved to Westminster, but because euthanasia falls with the criminal law, it may in fact be a devolved matter. It will fall within the ambit of those with ministerial responsibility for the criminal law and hence the decriminalisation of homicide on compassionate grounds is a devolved matter. It is difficult to imagine a situation in which different laws are allowed to operate north and south of the border.

### Active euthanasia

Although there are no reported Scottish cases in point, three crimes are relevant to active euthanasia: murder, culpable homicide and reckless endangerment of life. While euthanasia will amount to murder, because of the sympathy the facts may invoke, cases may be prosecuted as culpable homicide. Because the law distinguishes between intent and motive, a murder case may be established. While the intent will be consistent with murder, the motive may be altruistic. Such altruism would not affect the legal interpretation of the intent of the accused (*mens rea*), ie to bring about the death of another. The letter of the law does not always accord with its application. It is possible to find a body of largely unreported case law in which the elements of murder were present, but the charge was culpable homicide and the sentence was lenient following a guilty plea. This is because the mores of society may demand a certain level of flexibility in the common law. For example, in *HM Advocate* v *Brady* (1996), a man fed tranquilisers and alcohol to his brother who was suffering from end-stage Huntington's disease. It was found that this was done at the brother's earnest request. The court found Brady guilty of culpable homicide and admonished him.

As these cases often relate to terminal illnesses, the question arises of whether it makes any difference that the victim would have died anyway. The answer is that in law this makes no difference, as hastening the victim's death has no effect on the criminal nature of the act.

This is in contrast to the doctrine of "double effect" that applies to and admonishes medical practitioners, in which a palliative is administered even although it will hasten their death. It is perhaps for this reason that there has yet to be a prosecution of a medical practitioner in Scotland for murder by euthanasia. That said, where there is no therapeutic purpose to the treatment, a prosecution will follow. This is what happened in *R* v *Cox* (1992), where a lethal dose of potassium chloride was administered to a patient with a terminal illness who had expressed a wish to end her life. It was administered by her doctor, Dr Cox. His charge of murder was reduced to one of attempted murder, as the victim had been cremated and proof of the cause of death had become impossible to establish. He was convicted of the attempted murder.

## Passive euthanasia

An omission to treat leading to the death of the patient may amount to passive euthanasia. This will cover situations in which treatment is withdrawn from the patient in their best interests, as in the *Bland* and *Law Hospital* cases. These selective non-treatment cases should, however, be distinguished from those in which the patient elects non-treatment through a "do not resuscitate" order. Such orders were recognised as valid in *Re AK (Medical treatment: consent)* (2000) as long as steps have been taken to ensure that they reflect the true wishes of the patient. If it is possible to collapse the distinction between active and passive where the outcome is the same, this would mean that situations such as that in *Re AK* amount to physician–assisted suicide.

---

### Essential Facts

*Death in law*

- There is no statutory definition of death. It is generally accepted that brain stem death is the definitive medical usage.

*Futility and incapacity: children*

- "Futility" refers to demands by or on behalf of the patient for treatments that will not serve the desired medical ends or not be in the patient's best medical interests.
- English case law holds that respect is given by doctors and the courts for the views of parents for or against treatment, but the court's determination of the child's best interests is paramount. A doctor may not impose medical treatment in the face of parental objections.
- Courts weigh likely benefits of treatment from the child's point of view as if the court were the responsible parent.
- Courts have the role of resolving any conflict between medical professional opinion and parental wishes and will accept medical recommendations on prognosis and whether treatment is in the child's best interests.
- A court will not order that treatment be given where medical opinion holds it to be of no – or only short-term – benefit to the child, but will authorise treatment where there is not much pain or risk. It may do this in the face of parental objection.
- "Best interests" should include emotional and welfare interests as well as medical interests.
- There is a strong presumption in favour of life, which is rebuttable on the ground of best interests
- The European Convention on Human Rights has become the mechanism through which these scenarios are adjudicated, particularly Art 2 on the right to life, Art 3 prohibiting inhuman and degrading treatment and Art 8 on respect for private life.

*Futility and incapacity: adults*

- The appropriate test is one of "substituted judgement" in deciding whether to withhold or withdraw life-prolonging treatment from an adult in a permanent vegetative state (PVS).

- Before substituted judgement decisions are made, evidence is required from two independent medical practitioners that the patient is, in fact, in a PVS.

- Treatment may lawfully be withdrawn from a patient in PVS if it is in the patient's best medical interests where it is futile to prolong life, yet, according to the *Bland* and *Law Hospital* judgments, patients in a PVS do not have any best interests to protect.

- Withdrawal of treatment from a patient in a PVS will not be a criminal offence in the absence of a duty to act.

- Following the *Law Hospital* decision, the petitioner in future cases should lodge with the petition at least two medical reports on the patient's condition that describe the proposed course of action and the steps that will be taken to allow death to occur with dignity, a statement of the first diagnosis of PVS and a statement of any views on treatment decisions that the patient may have expressed prior to going into a PVS.

- As a civil court, it is not competent for the Court of Session to issue a declarator in respect of the criminal or otherwise nature of the withdrawal of medical treatment.

- The distinction between acts and omissions is an important policy device of the courts: omissions are permissible and acts may be culpable.

- There is authority under Part 5 of the Adults with Incapacity (Scotland) Act 2000 for the medical practitioner primarily responsible for the care of a patient to do what is reasonable in the circumstances in relation to medical treatment in order to safeguard the patient's physical and mental health. What is excluded from Part 5 is "negative" treatment.

*Advance statements*

- An advance statement on treatment decisions must be made when the patient is competent to do so and acted upon when the patient is no longer competent.

- There is judicial authority that advance statements are competent in some situations, but not legally binding if they run contrary to the patient's best interests or to the doctor's clinical judgement.
- The Mental Health (Care and Treatment) (Scotland) Act 2003 deals with advance directives only in respect of compulsory treatment. It sets out the form and procedure to be followed and the authority the statement will have.

*Assisted suicide*

- Killing a person at their request amounts to murder.
- Criminal liability may also be on the basis of culpable homicide or recklessly endangering life.
- The European Convention on Human Rights does not form the basis of assuring an applicant to the court that another person would not be prosecuted for helping them to die at the time of their choosing (her husband, in the case of Dianne Pretty, who suffered from motor neurone disease).
- Physician-assisted suicide is applied where, at the patient's request, a medical practitioner helps end the life of a patient who is incapable of doing so himself. The doctor may have recourse to the doctrine of double effect.

*Euthanasia*

- Euthanasia may be defined as putting someone to death in a compassionate manner following their suffering.
- As it falls within the criminal law, it is technically devolved to the Scottish Parliament.
- Three crimes are relevant to active euthanasia: murder, culpable homicide and reckless endangerment of life.
- Prosecutions and sentences tend to be lenient, based on culpable homicide rather than murder and not resulting in custodial sentences.
- Hastening the victim's death has no effect on the criminal nature of the act.
- Where there is no therapeutic purpose to the treatment, the doctrine of double effect will be unavailable to the accused and a prosecution will follow.

- Passive euthanasia is arguably no different to the position in the *Bland* and *Law Hospital* judgments.
- "Do not resuscitate" orders have been judicially recognised as valid if steps have been taken to ensure that they reflect the true wishes of the patient.

## Essential Cases

**Re B (a minor) (wardship: medical treatment) (1992)**: an operation on a child with Down's Syndrome to correct an intestinal condition could be performed, as the expected quality of life outweighed the destruction of life.

**Re J (a minor) (wardship: medical treatment) (1992)**: where a child was not dying but severely disabled, the court had to decide whether J should be revived should he collapse again. It was found that in the child's best interests, active steps to hasten death would not be authorised but it was not in the child's best interests to ventilate him if he was to stop breathing, unless it was considered medically appropriate to do so.

**Re C (a baby) (1996)**: where a baby became brain damaged from meningitis, the court approved of the medical expert agreement that it was not in her best interests to be ventilated artificially.

**A National Health Service Trust v D (2000)**: Art 2 of the ECHR on the right to life would not be infringed if non-treatment was in the child's best interests. Non-treatment protected the child from inhuman and degrading treatment under Art 3 of the ECHR as it was by its nature in her best medical interests.

**Glass v United Kingdom (2004)**: treatment contrary to parental wishes and without court authority to treat, violates Art 8 of the ECHR on respect for private life.

**Re A (children) (conjoined twins: surgical separation) (2000)**: two girls, conjoined twins, were considered separate persons. The benefits of separating them, giving the stronger twin continued life, outweighed the other's inevitable death. It was impossible to invoke the "best interests" test in respect of both girls; the court considered its decision in terms of the lesser of two evils. "Best interests' should include emotional and welfare interests as well as medical interests.